Brothers

from time to time

Emi Rivero, early 1950's

Adolfo Rivero, 1957

Brothers

from time to time

'I told them to shoot you.'
'And so you saved my life.'

By David Landau

Pureplay Press
San Francisco

First Edition

Brothers from time to time
Copyright © 2020 by David Landau
This edition © Pureplay Press

Subtitle by Harry Hurt, III
Text design by Ingrid Buuck
Covers by Naomi Hirooka

Photos without captions:
(front cover) Adolfo, *La vieja*, Emi, 1947
(courtesy page) Riverito in exile, 1959
(back cover) Malecón, Havana, 2002; author photo, 2018

Pureplay Press, San Francisco
www.pureplaypress.com
info@pureplaypress.com

Comments are welcomed. Notes about errors are especially appreciated.

ISBN 978-0-9765096-5-3

Principal subject headings: History – Cuba, Revolution, 1959 –
Family, Politics – Fidel Castro – United States, CIA

dedication

To a quartet of friends

Néstor Díaz de Villegas is a poet and essayist whose cycle of sonnets, P*or el camino de Sade*, I translated and published in 2002. Sixteen years later, with fire and conviction, he insisted that I return to an old subject and write this book. His mark is all over it.

Harry Hurt, III, a close friend from *Harvard Crimson* days, gave this book a crucial early affirmation. To the text, to the covers, to publishing strategy and to my own morale, his contributions have been signal.

Steve Hecht, whom I met in high school, has been an inseparable companion in Latin American matters for a quarter of a century. He is now publishing this book, in its two languages, on his website www.impunityobserver.com.

Kiko Arocha met Adolfo Rivero at Havana University in the 1950's. In 2020 Kiko delivered himself to the task of recreating, in Spanish, this history of Adolfo's family. "I have never felt so committed to doing a good job," he wrote to me at the start of his work, "because the two brothers will be looking over my shoulders."

As Harry Hurt says, your best friends are your oldest friends.

Brothers

from time to time

*A veces
perdiendo
se gana.*

"At times you lose
in order to win."

{Spanish proverb}

Part One

Regimes

The Rivero family

01

Nights in the gardens of Havana

At the start of many narratives you see the phrase, "inspired by a true story."

As it happens, every story on earth is a "true story." That includes the apocryphal story, which often has more value than the one governed by literal truth.

That said, the present work is a history which aims for literal truth. All the characters are portraits of actual people. No one is a composite. All bear the names to which they answered in life, including nicknames, pet names and underground names.

Almost everything here comes from direct experience and testimony of the main characters. Virtually all the dialogue is from first-hand accounts. Imagination is used to envision how things were; never to construct alternatives.

It's amazing how much apocryphal stuff makes its way into venerated works of history. And speaking of veneration, the only people in this tale who look for it are the heads of state who come and go.

The principal players were not heads of state or anything close. In life they had their dreams of glory. But now, if they could speak from the beyond, they would only ask for truth. Even in going for glory, they were obsessively faithful to facts. And they paid a high price for their scruples. The least one can do in a story about them is to apply the same standard.

§ § §

Havana, circa 1950. The photo above presents the four leading actors in this story, plus one other who will make a crucial contribution.

In the center is Adolfo Rivero Rodríguez (1904-1975), a Cuban newspaper correspondent who in 1950 is serving as head of the presidential press corps. Outside the family he is called "Riverito" – little Rivero – while within the family he is *viejo*, Dad.

Riverito has taken a long road to this table. He was born into a farming family in Camagüey province, with a father and sons tilling the land. The youngest of nine sons, little Rivero wished for another kind of life.

At age twelve – after a beating from his oldest brother, enforcing Father's will in the old-fashioned way – Riverito fled from home. Instead of coming back next day, he was gone. Only later did his family learn that he had crossed hundreds of miles to the dreamscape city of Havana, where he learned to be a productive citizen.

Riverito never broke with his family. In his early 20's he attended an older sister's wedding and fell for 15-year-old Delia Caro, daughter of the groom. Riverito and Delia were married and quickly joined by a son, Emi, who was born in the house of a former nemesis – Riverito's oldest brother.

Riverito took his young family to Havana, where he stood a better chance than in the depressed countryside. He earned a living as a photographer in the city's cafés, also running errands for a newspaper editor. In 1933 he landed a job as an assistant reporter at the Presidential Palace.

By 1950 Riverito is one of the country's leading journalists, a friend to presidents and to the major players in Cuban politics. In a short time, when he completes his term as chief of the presidential press corps, his fellow journalists will give him a plaque inscribed with his qualities – "dynamic, excitable, untiring, ready to serve."[1]

At Riverito's side in the photo is his wife Delia Caro Valdés (1912-1983), nearly always called *vieja* or Mom. Brilliant and beautiful, inspiring in her personal power, *la vieja* is the prime mover of her family; everyone cedes to her.

Next to *la vieja* is her younger son Adolfo Rivero Caro (1935-2011) – a lad by himself, gazing into the unknown. Shy and timid with a big ambition beneath, he is already placing bets for his father and uncle at Havana's *jai alai* matches. In a few years he will be a communist revolutionary.

Across from Adolfo is his elder brother and near-namesake Emilio Adolfo Rivero Caro, or Emi (1928-2016). An attorney and journalist, Emi is still in thrall to his father. But two years hence, when Batista seizes power in a *coup*, Emi will strike out on his own. At heart Riverito is a courtier while his older boy is an insurgent. Throughout the 1950's Emi will fight for Batista's overthrow. Starting in 1959, when a new ruler comes to power

---

[1] «Dinámico, nervioso, incansable, servicial»

in a *coup* and shows his colors, Emi will fight even harder to overthrow Fidel.

Next to Emi in the photo is his wife Lizbet – not her given name but the name of Nietzsche's sister, which Emi bestowed on her during their high-school romance. Now with a little Emi of their own, the two are gone from the world of gods and heroes and are smack in the middle of a young family's struggles.

A few years from now, with Adolfo joining the 'rejected sect' of communism and Emi vowing to "die in the street if necessary," Riverito and *la vieja* will wonder – in Emi's words – "Where do they come from, these beings to whom we gave life?"

They come from a vortex, yet unseen, that's about to devour their society.

02

The watchers

Under the Caribbean sky, thousands of people were watching you and you didn't see any of them – even if you had a vague sensation of being watched.

The watchers looked like everyday people in everyday clothes: young men in sports coats; two-hour women dressed like senators' wives; medical doctors in scrubs, bus drivers in uniform; professors or beach-combers, dressing as they liked; peanut vendors or local characters, every one a reassuring sight.

They worked wherever you worked; in offices or hospitals, on baseball teams or prison crews, at nightclubs or psychiatric wards; each of them distinct but with a signal commonality. Unbeknownst to you or almost anyone, the watchers were serving as agents of the revolutionary regime.

They saw themselves as citizens of the world's most advanced society. A pair of years earlier, their country had made a revolution *inside* the United States; for they, the people of Cuba, were American in all but name. But the US had answered their revolution by sending a so-called volunteer army of Cubans to topple it.

Against this attack the island nation had mustered a unique defense: it had used a people's army to beat back the invasion and humiliate the superpower. Its leaders also wielded a superb counterintelligence, with methods lent by Soviet spy agencies.

In the history of modern warfare, no adversary had given America such a drubbing; not the British Empire, not the Spanish Empire, not the Nazi behemoth or the land of the Rising Sun. And yet the tiny island nation, armed with little more than a newfound belief in itself, had done to America what those mighty powers had failed to do.

In an instant, Cuba was the mouse that roared. Its victory over the United States inspired awe throughout the hemisphere. Other nations turned to Cuba for help and advice. The Caribbean champion was quickly promoted to the front rank of global powers.

With all their success, Cuba's rulers poured on still more vigilance. The revolution was not out of danger. America was plotting a return engagement; while the new regime was facing enemies inside the country who were trying even harder to bring down the house.

{The following narrative is taken from recollections by Adolfo Rivero, who at age twenty-six was a senior official of Cuba's Communist Party and a leader of the regime's youth organizations.}

Havana, late summer 1961. I was about to leave Rebel Youth headquarters when I was told that two comrades wished to see me. It was odd because I didn't have office visits from strangers. In my work I dealt with Party officials and Party matters only. Anyone else wanting to raise a subject with me would have to contact the Party; and if I had to answer for anything, it would be a Party cadre who came and spoke with me.

Clearly the two comrades were exempt from those protocols. They wore civilian clothing. At a glance they appeared to be ordinary citizens; but their seriousness and their manner of looking at me showed that they were not quite ordinary.

They introduced themselves as being from State Security. They told me they were my brother's interrogators. No further identification was given and none was necessary.

One of them, the senior agent, carried the burden of conversation. He was tall, thin, and tired. He didn't waste words.

He said they needed my help in dealing with my brother.

"I feel sorry for you guys," I told them. "You've got a tough customer there." They gave a laugh of recognition; we knew we were talking about the same man.

I explained that my brother had fought against Batista's regime but in a group of bourgeois revolutionaries, the so-called Triple-A – people who didn't care for social reform and were only out for personal glory. My brother had wasted his energies with those fakes. If he had worked with Fidel he would have had contact with the peasant movement; or if he had worked with communists he would have learned about workers and the urban poor. But he rejected communism, and when the revolution came to power he rejected the leadership of Fidel. Worse than anything, he asked for help from the CIA and turned himself into an enemy agent. Those were the terrible choices that had led to his arrest.

"Yes, it is a pity," the senior agent said. "He is courageous."

I had little sympathy for that idea. Courage in a poor cause is nothing to admire. "To my brother, danger is a sport," I replied.

The senior man smiled and said, "He is very intelligent. We have been talking with him for many hours. He says he can reach Kennedy personally and mediate an agreement between Cuba and the US. Is it trustworthy, what he says? How would you evaluate it?"

I realized those men were in need of political guidance. I couldn't tell much about their formation but one thing I knew: they could not be communists. A communist would have known that any talk of a deal with Kennedy was nonsense. A communist would have had no doubts about what the struggle was or who the enemy was.

"My brother worships honor," I said with energy. "But that is not the issue. The issue is that my brother is a CIA agent. What agreement can possibly exist between the CIA and the revolution?"

The agents looked at me without uttering a word. Finally the senior man asked: "In your opinion, what should we do?"

I answered without blinking. "The revolution can have no deal with my brother – not now and not in the future. I believe you should execute him before a firing squad."

The senior man and I stood looking into each other's eyes. It seemed to me that for an instant he couldn't meet my gaze.

"Thanks," he said. "We will see each other again soon."

We shook hands and they left. They never came back. For 27 years I spoke with no one about this conversation, except with my comrade César Gómez a few days afterward.

"You did right," my closest friend told me. "I would have done the same."[2]

---

[2] A version of this narrative appears in Adolfo Rivero Caro & Emilio Adolfo Rivero Caro, *Las cabañitas/The Little Cabins,* Miami: Alexandria Library, 2012 (twin Spanish and English volumes).

03

We need a revolution

{from Adolfo Rivero's recollections}

Havana, spring 1954. My brother and I didn't see each other too often. Between his addiction to work, which we all knew, and his conspiring, which we took for granted, Emi was out of our sight for long periods of time.

One morning in April or May 1954 I had come back from the university and was in my room, reading a communist pamphlet on US companies in Cuba. As usual the arguments were solid, the figures objective, the conclusions distressing. Once more I had to ask myself: If the basic parts of our economy were held by American companies, then who owned the country? If the answer was "Americans," as it surely must be, then how independent was Cuba? It seemed we were not a free country at all but still a colony.

In their political talk Cubans were saying: Batista is wrong, Batista is evil, we have to get rid of Batista. But if Cuba was owned by Americans, what difference would it make if someone else was president?

Almost nobody seemed to notice this problem. Many talked about "revolution." Some were even willing to fight for it. Not many however could say what this "revolution" would do except get rid of Batista. The only ones who saw the problem in its actual size, who talked about changes that could matter, were the communists.

The question before me as I read that communist pamphlet was not its argument, which I knew to be valid, but rather its meaning for me. What would be my part in these coming changes? What could I do? What must I do?

Usually my father came to lunch at around one. That day for some reason he came earlier and with my brother. When they entered the house I was deep in thought. My room was very hot and I had put on the air conditioning.

"Workers of the world, unite!" Emi belted out as he walked in.

My brother's manner often had the effect of putting me on edge. Even more, I inferred from his greeting that our mother was telling him about me. For months now she had been finding Communist Party leaflets in my room and strongly disapproved.

I got up to greet Emi, leaving my pamphlet on the bed where I hoped he wouldn't notice it.

He took off his watch and showed it to me. "A Movado; it's new, solid gold. How do you like it?"

"It's fine," I said without enthusiasm.

"I'm wearing it so I can know the exact time of Batista's downfall," he said, giving voice to his obsession. Then he picked up the pamphlet I had dropped on the bed. "Trash," he said and dropped it back.

"Not so, brother! Facts. Reality. The unfortunate truth."

"I understand how a black man in a shantytown or a farm worker who cuts cane becomes a communist. But you. You!"

Yes! I, Adolfo Rivero, communist! It made all the sense in the world.

{from Emi's & Adolfo's recollections}

Emi smiled at his younger brother, speaking tenderly. "Look Adolfito, the Americans are not to blame for that. If you want to blame anyone, blame the Cubans who sold to them. American companies do business, not philanthropy. You might not like it but it's hardly criminal."

"Then the system is criminal for letting the rich always prevail!"

"That's incorrect. Labor unions are very powerful in the United States, and here too."

"Powerful to win alms," Adolfo countered.

"Not alms. Good wages, living standards – everything they want."

"No, not everything! Not by any means. Workers must control what they produce. They are the rightful masters of society!"

"What makes you say that?" Emi asked. "Workers have never ruled any society in history."

"What about the Soviet Union?"

"The Soviet Union is ruled by the Communist Party."

"And whom does the Party represent, if not the workers?"

"The Party represents itself. Its goal is to keep power for itself."

"You and your friends are out for glory!" Adolfo charged. "You don't care about changing society at all!"

"Changing society yes, by all means. But change within the rules of democracy. Freedom is the most important thing."

"Freedom is a clever illusion," Adolfo said dismissively. "What good is freedom without the possibility of change?"

"The communists don't care about freedom – or perhaps they do. They hate freedom and would like to take it away."

La vieja came into the room. "What is all this hollering?"

"Adolfito is the only one hollering," Emi said calmly.

"Wash your hands," *la vieja* said. "The table is being set."

"I'm not hungry!" Adolfo exclaimed.

"Don't make your father wait," she said.

When the old man saw them coming, he put down his newspaper and went to sit at the head of the table.

Percy the cook overextended herself when Emi came, and Emi flattered her without remorse. "Old man," Emi said to *el viejo* as Percy brought more food, "if I give you my car, would you allow Percy to come and work at my place?"

"I'm not interested in your car," the old man said with a smile. "As for the rest, that's Percy's problem."

"I'm very happy here," the attractive mulatto girl said melodically. "If you are not satisfied at home, come to eat here more often." She spoke like a member of the family.

"Good idea," Emi said, piling up extra portions.

"What was all that hollering?" *el viejo* asked.

"Nothing, a brotherly discussion," Emi said. "It seems Adolfito is interested in communism. It's become a fad at the university."

"It is not a fad at the university! And I do not go in for fads or brands or watches or cars or anything of the kind!"

"Don't brag about your lack of discrimination," Emi said.

"I know all the leaders of the Communist Party," the old man put in. "They're friends of mine. They are more Cuban than communist, in my opinion." He spoke nonchalantly, trying to nudge the matter away.

Emi looked at his brother's plate. "That meal you are eating is not a proletarian meal."

"No, but I would like it to be."

"Oh, my son," *la vieja* broke in, telling Adolfo what her husband had not, "if the communists succeed here, we are going to have such a hunger!"

"Let's get going," the old man said. "I have to put gas in the car."

"Máximo's station is closed," Emi said.

"Máximo closed?" the old man said lightly. "We need a revolution."

04

Keep up your guard

{from Emi Rivero's recollections}

Havana. On May 1, 1953 my disgrace was complete; Lizbet and I were divorced. I moved to an apartment house at 19th and O, a building I called "The Castle." It was diagonal to the Hotel Nacional; my room obliquely faced the sea.

A year after the coup that had removed President Carlos Prío from office, Batista's regime was openly illegal. People had no freedom to challenge it. They could go about their lives, but if they said a word against the government they paid a price.

Corruption was unbelievable. My father was on close terms with Batista's personal minister.[3] He had the right to knock at the man's private door and enter without waiting for a response. One time he found the minister with stacks of thousand-dollar bills. "Come in Riverito, sit down, wait a minute." The man was counting out millions of dollars in payoffs.

Every prostitute in Cuba, thousands of women, had to give a dollar a day to the police. That money was cut into different parts: one for the president of the republic, one for the first lady, one for the police chief, one for the precinct captain, one for the police officer. The beat cop who earned $120 a month and collected from a hundred prostitutes was allowed to keep a nickel of every dollar – $5 a day, the same as his official salary.

---

[3] Andrés Domingo y Morales del Castillo

The parking meters were run by the president's brother-in-law who was also an army general. But even in Batista's time Cuba was cleaner than other Latin countries. In Cuba they grafted a percent of each public-works project before the work was done. In other countries they grafted a bigger percent of the money and the work was not done.

Most Cubans, while intensely disliking Batista, put up with his rule. A minority however did not. I rejected it completely and joined the Triple-A. This group, led by Prío's former minister Aureliano Sánchez, was dedicated to restoring Cuba's constitution and freedoms.[4]

Meeting his group at a restaurant, Emi saw Armando Franco and held out a hand. With a rapid motion Armando reached past Emi's hand, grabbed his testicles and yanked downward. As Emi swooned, Armando laughed and crossed his hands over his groin.

"Why do you do that?" Emi said to the crossed hands. "Do you think I'm so stupid as to try a counterstrike now?"

Whenever they met after that, Armando crossed his hands over his groin. A conspirator's first rule: Keep up your guard.

Armando was in charge of the Triple-A shock troops. The Triple-A was unfolding plans for a coup of its own. They were smuggling large quantities of arms into Cuba and forming action groups among civilians as well as military. They kept tabs on the regime through informants of their own. Emi, who could handle guns, worked under Armando as an arms carrier and weapons trainer.

Emi's phone rang after two in the morning. "Rivero." It was Armando's voice, low and resolute. "Meet me at three, where the bread chases the dog."

---

[4] The name 'Triple-A' stood for *Asociación de Amigos de Aureliano* – Association of Aureliano's Friends.

That was a popular hamburger stand whose immense neon sign showed a bread-roll trying to capture a dog. Hardly had Emi's car stopped under the sign when agents of the SIM, Batista's military intelligence, pulled up behind him.

"Out of the car!" they snapped.

As they inspected his car Emi heard the unmistakable sound of Armando's Ford, badly needing a muffler. "Stay away from here!" Emi thought to himself.

Armando entered the circle and kept coming closer. Didn't he see the police? Armando pulled up and parked right behind the SIM car.

The agents fell on the Ford and searched it thoroughly. "Hmmm! What's this?"

It was fishing gear.

Once the agents had left, Armando smiled. "Okay! Today we go fishing." They drove out of the city to a favorite spot and fished. As he cooled down, Emi realized that Armando had been testing him.

My Triple-A partner Carlos Manuel Malgrat was a psychologist who worked in crisis services. He was mid-30's, ten years older than I; thin and brawny with crew-cut blond hair, green slanted eyes above high cheekbones and an odd, ringing laugh.

"When the egg hits the rock it's bad for the egg. When the rock hits the egg it's bad for the egg. We are the eggs," Malgrat used to say about himself and his comrades.

Malgrat lived with his mother and a ten-year-old half-sister whom he evidently supported. He also had a bachelor's apartment that the Triple-A used as a cache for weapons, explosives, police uniforms and documents.

On a warm day Emi had carried a 50-pound box of dynamite into the place. The dynamite was sweating through the box. Not familiar with the chemistry of explosives, the two men thought they must keep the dynamite cool; so they hurried out to buy a fan and blew air on the box until the sweating stopped.

Whenever Malgrat was going to have a girl in the place he slid the box under the bed. "Imagine!" Emi told him. "If this goes off the girl will find herself in heaven or hell and she will be thinking: What a man! What a man! I never had an orgasm like this!"

Malgrat was choking with laughter. "And can you imagine the poor Spaniard who has worked and saved all his life to build these apartments? In an instant, ka-BOOM! And probably he's such a cheapskate that the building is not even insured!"

That kind of horseplay was unusual for Malgrat. He did everything right, with no wasted motion. Where Armando was neurotic and sloppy, Malgrat was disciplined and savvy. Brave, loyal, *simpático* Armando was a pain in the ass, while Malgrat fit every situation like a glove.

The Triple-A suffered a massive breach of security when SIM agents raided a residence and captured, among other things, a list of conspirators. Shortly afterward Batista's men rudely entered the press room of the Presidential Palace, a sacrosanct area, and arrested a journalist. Other conspirators were being arrested in their homes or picked off the streets.

The Triple-A was in chaos. Its leaders hurried into hiding or ran to embassies. Armando, Emi, Malgrat and their peers would be the SIM's next targets, but they could not think of running; they must stand their ground and keep visible so their scattered comrades would have a focus for regrouping.

Riverito showed up at his son's place. He was there to take Emi to Jorge Quintana, dean of the Cuban journalists' guild and one of his father's innumerable friends. "He'll arrange your asylum in the Mexican embassy."

"I'm not going into any embassy!" Emi roared. "If I have to, I'll die in the street!"

"So this is what I have to deal with!" the old man thought.

§§§

"Fifth and E Streets?" I asked, hoping I'd misunderstood.

"No, Fifth and G, as in García, Salvador Díaz Versón corrected me. "Police raided the apartment yesterday. They found documents, police uniforms, explosives. They arrested a man and put him in a specially guarded cell. No one can get to him or get information about his case, not even high officers. He must have been severely beaten."

That was Malgrat's apartment. Malgrat had to be the one in that cell. Why the security measures? How badly had they hurt him?

That wasn't all. As he looked at the man in front of him, Emi had a single thought: *Salvador, you are dead. I know it for a fact, and I'm not allowed to tell you.*

Salvador, a veteran intelligence man, had been second in command of the SIM under Prío. After the *coup* he offered his services to the Triple-A. Emi was assigned as liaison to Salvador with an unusual proviso: Don't tell him anything, just take information. Always be a catcher with him, never a pitcher.

The target of this restriction was not Salvador but the US embassy. Salvador's links to the embassy were close, going back to World War II and before. Intelligence agents like to chew each other's ears without regard to politics or regimes. Surely Salvador talked with the Americans. Since the US gave pivotal support to Batista's regime, Triple-A leaders wanted to make sure no one in the US embassy would hear about their operations or plans.

Salvador raised no questions with Emi. He simply gave his reports while the younger man listened. Emi typed up his reports and sent them unsigned to the Triple-A secretariat. Copies of his memos, referring to information from "S.D.V.," would have been at Malgrat's place. Police were now holding those copies.

What should Emi do? Warn Salvador, or keep his promise to catch and not pitch?

Those were agonizing minutes, thinking that probably in a few hours this man would be arrested, perhaps tortured or killed, as a result of events he himself was disclosing to me. I was the only one who could prevent his arrest. But I had no question about what I must do. My instructions on this point had been very clear. I didn't tell him anything.

Shortly after seeing Emi, Salvador was arrested at home and taken under guard to military intelligence. His interrogator, a colonel, was the man who had succeeded him as deputy chief.

Salvador vehemently denied being S.D.V. "Listen," he told the colonel. "You and I are very good friends. You are an old officer, I am an old officer. You know that coincidences occur and that we are misled by them."

At that moment Salvador began to have trouble breathing. He had a heart problem of which the colonel was aware. As his breathing worsened, everyone got concerned. "We can't have him die in here!" they thought.

"Okay," the colonel said, "I'm sending you home under house arrest."

They calmed him down and drove him home. Salvador lived in a *quinta*, a country place in an outlying district. Next day he wandered out to the orchard, waited for the guards to turn their backs, went over a fence and made his way to the center of town, where he took refuge in an embassy.

When the colonel called Salvador's house to speak with him, Salvador's wife, whose canniness matched her husband's, told him: "But colonel, don't you know? He's in an embassy!"

"¡Señora!" the colonel replied, extremely flustered. "Do you understand the position in which your husband has placed me before the President of the Republic?"

"My husband was terrified of you! He went to the embassy because he thought you were going to kill him!" she said – and wasted no time joining her husband.

Though his poise and wit enabled him to escape, I still feel guilt before his memory, before his family. I'm convinced that if our roles had been reversed, Salvador would have told me to run.[5]

The Triple-A had many informants in the police. Those people avoided direct contact with us and used cut-outs instead. Mariano Posada was taller than average, lean, balding and notably dignified. He had a circumspect, prudent attitude like that of the businessman he probably was.

Mariano summoned Emi to a meeting and began to deliver a piece of news in a plain, somber tone. Emi had never seen him so concerned.

"A man arrested by police nine days ago identified himself as working for the Palace's secret service." Mariano said. "The man is between thirty and forty, blond, crew-cut, prominent cheek bones, about your height. He has an apartment at Fifth and G."

That could only be Malgrat. "Are you sure?" Emi asked as pressure built up in his temples.

"The driver of the car that took him to the bureau is an informant of ours. He said the arrested man identified himself as secret service while still in the car."

---

[5] Further information about S.D.V. comes from a profile that was apparently created in Florida during the early days of the Castro regime: http://cuban-exile.com/doc_326-350/doc0345.html

So! Malgrat was in an isolated cell not because he had been beaten or tortured but because he worked for Batista.

Police had gone to his place on a tip and struck gold – finding, along with the man, documents, police uniforms, weapons and dynamite. Malgrat knew how the arresting officers would treat him. They would try to extract information quickly and by most unpleasant means. He must establish his identity as a presidential agent before getting to the station, where horrors awaited him.

"Here!" he told the men in the car. "Call this number. They'll tell you!"

The driver confirmed Malgrat's identity as a Batista agent. No one knew the driver himself was a Triple-A informant.

Getting the truth about Malgrat gave some satisfaction but Emi now had much bigger concerns. He turned abruptly to go, forgetting the handshake.

Mariano did not want Emi to leave that way. He grabbed his arm and said: "You! You! What are you going to do?"

"I don't know," Emi mumbled and went.

At home he waited for police to arrive. He waited and waited. They didn't come. Why? Before arresting Riverito's son they would have to be sure. But now they were sure.

What was keeping them? Malgrat had been closer to him than to anyone. Emi should have been their first order of business. It was ten days and counting. What made them wait?

Armando was arrested. They put him in the "Vivac," their first stop for political detainees.

A message came down to Emi from the Triple-A leaders. "We must make contact with Armando. None of us can visit him. You're a lawyer. Present yourself at the Vivac and ask to see him.

Someone will wait for you outside the prison. If they have a tight surveillance of him and you're arrested, we'll notify your father immediately."

In plain language, they wanted to know whether Armando had talked.

Emi reasoned: *If police haven't come for me here, no one will bother me at the Vivac.* At once he went to the prison and demanded to see Armando.

He was shown to a divider made of wooden bars. Behind the bars was an office, and at the back of the office a barred iron door before a long corridor of cells. An officer went to the iron door and yelled: "¡Armando Perfecto Franco Mainier!"

A guard led a prisoner along that corridor toward the iron door. Emi saw a sick old man being brought toward him. Armando shuffled slowly, with serious difficulty. As he was brought through the gate Armando looked up at Emi, smiled and crossed his hands over his groin.

Emi felt his eyes water. *Stay calm!* He ordered himself. *Don't show them anything!*

Armando came closer and held his right hand out to Emi through the wooden bars, while keeping the left hand over his groin. His neck had heavy bruises and scratches. His eyes were bloodshot; he was drained and haggard.

"They took me from María's" – his mistress, a nurse who lived with her two kids in a shantytown. "When they led me from the house a cop was yelling: 'To that car! To that car! Not to the other car!'"

Malgrat was in the other car – to finger him.

"How are you feeling?" Emi asked.

"I think some ribs are broken. My balls are twice their normal size. They almost strangled me with barbed wire." He smiled and shrugged. "Someone wanted information on matters about which I know nothing."

Armando got a six-year sentence. Malgrat left prison after a short term and went out of Cuba through the embassy of Panama – a move to keep up appearances.[6]

§§§

Some months later, in the spring of 1955, President Batista – apparently confident that the insurrection was over, and wishing for people to see him as a benevolent ruler – proclaimed a general amnesty. Armando went out of jail along with many who had raised their hands against the regime. One of those was Fidel Castro, who had served just 14 months for having led an armed attack on an army barracks at a cost of more than 50 lives.[7]

Following the amnesty Malgrat was free to visit from Panama, where he had apparently settled. Armando caught sight of him in a Havana restaurant with his mother and little sister, enjoying a side of beef. Armando watched for a minute, went back to his friends and exclaimed: "The fucker was eating one of my ribs!"

Emi was never arrested by Batista's police. He never understood why. After much rumination he could only suppose that Malgrat had genuinely liked him and preferred not to mess up his life. Malgrat would produce for the regime and earn his money, but he was no fanatic.

Emi realized he had saved his life simply by being himself. As the

---

[6] A thumbnail on Malgrat, published in Panama, documents his exit from Cuba without mentioning his counterintelligence work: <bdigital.binal.ac.pa/BIOVIC/Captura/upload/CarlosMMalgratG>.
[7] The Moncada attack of July 26, 1953, which marked the beginning of the Castro legend

lesson sank in, he took its measure. Even in the hard business of espionage, reprieves like this are sometimes granted. They are precious and surprising. They resist explanation. Like all things, they are temporary. But they do not happen by accident.

05

Winds of change

1954-1956. Havana University was the ratchet-wheel of Cuban politics; it cranked out protest after protest with increasing vehemence. Any occasion at all – the anniversary of a rebellion, the birthday of a national hero or a slain martyr – was enough to bring a student mob surging into the streets, crying for Batista's head.

Students and police became mortal enemies. Owing to an ancient restriction that even despots did not violate, police did not go onto campus. Instead they waited on nearby streets for protest groups to move into the city, where police could act freely. Every student march took the same route: down the big staircase to the main gate at L Street, then onto San Lázaro where police were waiting at the corner of Infanta.

Police opened fire. I looked to the side and saw my comrade on the ground, struck by a bullet.

Adolfo turned this experience into a short story which he shared with the family. Emi was hugely impressed, while the old ones were mortified. *El viejo*, sitting in the Presidential Palace, got wind of another student march about to begin. He grabbed his coat with a revolver inside and drove toward the university, leaving his car a few streets from where he knew police would be. The march ended without incident. Adolfo never knew that the old man had been close by, armed and ready to come to his aid.

Through a family member and on short notice, *el viejo* arranged for Adolfo to spend a year at Georgetown University in Washington DC instead of at Havana, where he would have been a junior. In the old man's experience Cuban political phenomena

were short-lived; he was betting the troubles would die down
before Adolfo's return.

Adolfo grabbed for the opportunity. It gave him a year at one
of the world's premier centers of learning. It also built in him a
magisterial capacity for the English language that would never
decline. In gratitude, Adolfo wrote to his father on the occasion
of the old man's 50th birthday:

"Today I remember you with the fidelity that distance alone can
offer; in your unceasing industry, your fantastic energy, your
eternal ability to put a smile on others' faces. I see you, in the
daily battle for life, tumble down a thousand times and suffer not
a little, but unfailingly, once and once again, pick yourself up,
repair your dented armor and renew the attack, brimming with
a fervor and optimism that only come to the young – and for
that, dear father, I raise a glass to your unconquerable freshness of
spirit, a greeting from one who remembers you with the fidelity
that distance alone can offer: your son Adolfo."

El viejo lost his bet about the political crisis and its duration.
When Adolfo returned to Havana University in mid-1955, more
than ever the business of "the hill" was Batista. At the end of 1955
the powerful student union, FEU, spawned a political arm, the
Directorio Revolucionario – 'Directorio' for short – whose purpose
was to join ranks with groups off the hill in an effort to depose
the president.

In his studies at Georgetown, Adolfo had examined the sources of
Marxism and had seen discrepancies that gave him pause about
communism. But the Cuban Communist Party (called *Partido
Socialista Popular*, or PSP) showed a clarity and audacity in direct
political work that appealed to him strongly. So he came closer to
the Party without yet taking the leap and joining it.

At the end of 1956 the FEU – whose word on campus was law –
voted to suspend all university activity until the end of Batista's
rule. Under the FEU's ruling, students could not work on their
degree-courses or be graduated. Only a few buildings remained

open for student meetings. Those students who had come to
university for the normal purpose of advancing their lives were
dealt a heavy blow. Batista and his cohorts, however, only gained
from the suspension; a large pot whose boiling they couldn't
control was suddenly off the stove.

§§§

1956-1957. The winds of change were shifting. Emi Rivero's
beloved Triple-A was stuck in a subroutine. Its leaders were
old-fashioned *caballeros* plotting on a human scale. They
were troubled by ethical dilemmas. They didn't want to hurt
a bystander. Aiming to do things perfectly, they did little or
nothing.

Fidel Castro on the other hand was an entrepreneur in search of
his moment. He and some 80 men under his command set sail
from Mexico on a yacht called *Granma*. The tiny armed force,
which its leader had dubbed the July 26th Movement,[8] reached
Oriente province, eastern Cuba, four days behind schedule and
put down in the wrong place.

A group of July 26th followers under 21-year-old Frank País,
acting separately from Castro, had already seized key buildings in
nearby Santiago de Cuba, the island's second city, and held them
for nearly a day. In official quarters the País uprising raised greater
concern than did Castro's gang. But both developments caught
the fancy of rebels in the capital who now looked with interest at
eastern Cuba.

Still attuned to Havana, Emi Rivero heard whispers that
the Directorio was plotting something big. He guessed the
Presidential Palace might be a target. As the Palace pressroom was
his father's second home, Emi saw fit to warn him.

---

[8] After the Moncada army barracks attack of July 26, 1953

"*¡Viejo!* Watch out! Don't stay at the Palace any longer than you need to. When you stop working, just get away from there."

"What are you talking about?" *el viejo* said sharply. After his shift Riverito liked to stay behind and socialize with his fellow journalists.

"Something is cooking. I'm not sure what. But we live in convulsive times, and you never know."

"Tall stories! And if one of them turns out to be true, we want to be there to report it."

One of the world's premier newspapers was about to add a tall story of its own. As of February 1957 Castro's ranks had thinned to just 18 men, scantily clad and poorly armed. Those men busied themselves making raids on army outposts or into local villages. The loan of a few blankets from a peasant, or the capture of three rifles from the army, made a difference in Fidel's fortunes.

But the *guerrilla* force had something bigger; it had Fidel's mastery in the art of appearances. Through friends of his movement with contacts in the Havana bureau of *The New York Times*, Castro managed to arrange a visit to his camp by a senior *Times* correspondent, Herbert L. Matthews, who trooped all the way from New York to verify reports of a "rebel army" operating in the hills of eastern Cuba.

Out of his visit Matthews fashioned a three-part series around an assertion that was ridiculous or prophetic, or both: "From the looks of things, General Batista cannot hope to suppress the Castro revolt."

Fidel's brother Raúl, who managed the tiny force, paraded his troops in front of Matthews using the same men again and again, to create the impression that Fidel commanded hundreds. Through Matthews and *The Times*, Fidel was able to tell Americans: "You can be sure that we have no animosity towards the United States . . . [We] are fighting for a democratic Cuba and an end to the dictatorship." As for Fidel himself, he drove a phalanx right into the old reporter's heart. "The personality of the man is overpowering," Matthews wrote. "It was easy to see that his men adored him . . . ."[9]

Matthews's reports in *The Times* turned Fidel into an international figure and the unique symbol of resistance to Batista. In Cuba Fidel's sudden prominence had a special impact on members of the Directorio, who felt they must act before Castro preempted them.

"¡*Viejo!* Are you watching out?" Emi Rivero kept asking his father. "Leaving the Palace when your shift is over?"

"Fuck it, said the duchess! How many times do you have to say the same thing?"

In the Palace pressroom on a midweek afternoon, a group of men seated round a table were playing cards when the telephone rang. Riverito picked it up.

"Listen Riverito, this is *Tiempo en Cuba*.[10] Is it true the Presidential Palace is under attack?"

"Don't talk shit, boy!" And the receiver went slamming down.

Almost before they knew it, Riverito and his pals dropped to the floor as machine-guns blasted from a few yards away. A small army of men in blue trousers and white shirts was charging at the Palace, firing on the president's guards.[11] The reporters crawled to the back of the pressroom and into the WC, where a woman journalist kept muttering: "May the Holy Virgin protect us with her robe!"

---

[9] *The New York Times*, February 24, 1957, p. 1 & ff.
[10] A pro-Batista newspaper
[11] The trousers had been chosen to look like those worn by police.

March 13, 1957, 3:30 p.m. The Directorio was attacking the Palace in broad daylight, on a busy weekday afternoon. Even before the small army had invaded the Palace grounds, a group led by student militant José Antonio Echeverría had seized the popular "Clock Radio" station and Echeverría had announced: "People of Cuba! At this moment the dictator Fulgencio Batista has just been executed in revolutionary fashion. . . ."

The trucks and cars taking Echeverría's comrades to the Palace had been held up in traffic, so the victory proclamation had gone on air even before the attack began; hence the call to the reporters' room and Riverito's terse reply. Even so, the attackers had caught the garrison by surprise and killed several guards on the spot. In minutes an immense cordon of soldiers and police had ringed the Palace; a second wave of men who had come to join the attack did not get near the Palace grounds.

Fighting was fierce. Attackers invaded Batista's second-floor offices only to find them empty. The canny ruler had jumped up to his living quarters on the floor above, taking a complement of riflemen with him. The only access to this floor was by an elevator already upstairs. The attackers were trapped between Batista's men firing from above and the armed force firing from below.

During the attack Riverito crawled out of the WC, reached a telephone and called *la vieja*, who happened to be at a clinic recovering from a hysterectomy. "*My*, don't worry, I'm fine," he told her. The English word "My" was their pet name for each other.

Emi was at his law office in Old Havana when he heard people buzzing about the attack. He found a friend and they got to a portico near the Palace, where people were watching from a protected area under a colonnade.

The attackers, having gained a first advantage, were overwhelmed by numbers. Across town in the streets near the university, student leader Echeverría was cut down by police. By late afternoon some 35 attackers and five Palace guards had lost their lives.

From his mountain hideout Fidel Castro bluntly called the attack "a useless expenditure of blood." For the Directorio it had been a heart-rending defeat.

That evening Emi saw his parents at the clinic where *la vieja* was staying. The old man was in shock; not from fear, but from having seen Batista's men go round to the attackers who lay wounded on the Palace grounds and shoot them dead rather than take them into custody.

"That was a massacre!" *el viejo* exclaimed. Emi was proud to find his father appalled and not afraid.

06

Self-sufficient

Southern Oriente province, mid-1957. Castro's July 26th forces attacked an outpost of the guardia rural or local militia in the town of El Uvero. Fidel's publicity machine trumpeted the attack as a major victory against the army. It was little more than a skirmish with provincial police. But Batista's government played into Castro's hands when it ordered the removal of peasants from areas in which rebels were active. That move created sympathy for the rebels and added to Castro's prestige.

Support for the July 26th Movement rose up in many towns across Cuba. Through June and July bombs went off, schools were set on fire, gunfights broke out and murders committed in the name of the July 26th program. Apart from the ouster of Batista, the contents of that program were unspecified; but the July 26th drew strength from Batista's repressive measures, which gave all the revolutionary theater Fidel needed.

A new US ambassador, Earl Smith, reached Havana in mid-July and promptly announced he would visit Oriente – site of the US naval base at Guantánamo and of the largest *yanqui* enterprises on the island. In an effort to control opposition before the ambassador's visit, Batista's police arrested 200 people and made a huge catch. Frank País, the young organizer who had led the uprising in Santiago at the time of the *Granma's* landing, was tracked from hideout to hideout before being shot dead in an alleyway.

As news of the killing spread, a general strike broke out in Santiago. Ambassador Smith, arriving in Santiago the day of País's funeral, encountered a large and noisy demonstration of women organized by *comandante* Pastora Núñez. Police ushered the ambassador and his wife into the town hall before beating back the women with truncheons and fire hoses. The ambassador, shocked by this official violence, talked to newsmen and called the police conduct "abhorrent."[12] As the body of Frank País was borne to its burial in a huge procession, the ambassador placed a wreath at the grave of Cuba's patriarch, José Martí.

By now Adolfo Rivero was much more deeply involved in clandestine work than his older brother. He had joined the Communist Party and become a wanted man. Everywhere outside his father's house, he was 'Félix' – his underground name and badge of honor.

In Félix's cell of the Socialist Youth,[13] a fierce debate was unfolding over how the party ought to relate to Castro's campaign.

"What's the point of going to the Sierra Maestra? The real fight is in Havana," one cadre asserted.

"The point is to show solidarity with the July 26th campaign," another cadre said.

"You mean join the *guerrilla* army? Or send supplies like medicines?"

---

[12] The Batista government nearly expelled Ambassador Smith in this dispute; see https://history.state.gov/historicaldocuments/frus1958-60v06/d189

[13] In Cuban political parlance, the terms 'socialist' and 'communist' have been used fairly interchangeably. The Communist Party, prior to Fidel's re-fashioning in the mid-60's, was called *Partido Socialista Popular* or People's Socialist Party. The PSP dated to the mid-1920's; communist old-timers like Aníbal Escalante, Fabio Grobart and Carlos Rafael Rodríguez were all formed in the PSP. As for the Party's youth organization, it changed names constantly. When Adolfo joined the Party as Félix, he went into the Socialist Youth or *Juventud socialista*. After Fidel's takeover in 1959 it became the Rebel Youth, *Juventud rebelde*. In 1963, as Fidel was turning the Party into an instrument of his personal power, it became the Communist Youth, *Juventud comunista*. During Adolfo's lifetime, popular jargon unified these different identities in at least one recognizable term: *ñángara* or 'commie.'

"Look!" a fellow called Felipe said. "At home I've got lots of medicines in a cardboard box. I would like to take them to the Sierra Maestra myself!"

"You are talking like a petit-bourgeois!" the general secretary of the cell said scornfully. "Here we do not behave in an individualistic fashion. We act as Party cadres."

"I don't go along with that," said César Gómez, a pal of Félix's from the university. "If we're going to find out what's best for the party and the revolution, we've got to think for ourselves. Isn't that what Nikita's reforms are all about?" he asked pointedly, speaking of Khrushchev's efforts to make the Soviet Communist Party more democratic.

César's independent streak was a trait that Party regulars derided with the stock term "self-sufficiency." Félix admired the trait even when he didn't share the opinion.

"Sorry César, I know the *guerrilla* campaign looks exciting but I don't think we're going anywhere with it," Félix said with a smile. "I think it will be mass actions that win the day, not attacks on remote outposts."

"One more thing," Felipe said.

"Go ahead," the general secretary allowed.

"The police keep coming to my place."

"Then don't go there."

"What about my mother?"

"*¡Coño, chico!* Do you want them to catch you? Don't go back to your house – ever!"

Unhappily it was good advice. A few days later police arrested Felipe in front of his house and killed him.

Félix, César and others in their group decided to organize a march in honor of Martí's birthday, January 28, 1958. Félix prepared leaflets while others made a banner 20 feet long. The group met at the corner of Galiano and San José, one of Havana's busiest intersections, at the height of the rush hour. They unfurled the huge banner and went running down Galiano with shouts of "*¡Abajo Batista!*"[14]

Félix handed leaflets to bystanders or just threw them into the air. The group charged toward San Rafael and picked up supporters, becoming a real crowd. Police counterattacked with raised clubs and revolvers, blowing their whistles furiously. The marchers ran in all directions, trying to blend in with the crowd. Félix walked along nervously, his pockets bulging with leaflets. If police picked him up he would be in serious trouble.

Two blocks later he found César walking in front of him, looking tense and suspicious. Félix thought his friend would not escape arrest. Just then he felt a grip on his arm like pliers. A big black man had come from out of nowhere and was holding him.

"Where are you going?" the plainclothes policeman said. "You were in the demonstration!"

"What demonstration?" Félix said indignantly. "I've just come out of the Minerva bookstore. I was even arguing with a clerk in there. Let's go and confirm it!"

The public hated Batista's men so much that if Félix and the officer had gone into the bookstore, any clerk would have backed up the story. The policeman, stung by Félix's upper-class manner, hesitated.

"Good Lord!" Félix said with annoyance. "Even peaceful citizens who enjoy reading have to put up with trouble from the police!"

---

[14] "Down with Batista!"

The policeman let him go.

When Félix got home and took off his shirt, his mother asked: "What's that?"

To Félix's surprise, the marks made by the other man's fingers were still on his arm. He laughed it off.

"That was a policeman," *la vieja* said without any logic at all.

07

A perfect squeeze

April 9, 1958, 11 a.m. Unidentified persons in Havana seized three radio stations and declared an emergency.

"Strike! Strike! Strike! Everyone on strike! Everyone into the streets! People of Cuba, the hour has struck! We must stop the tyranny of Batista, backed by the terror of thugs and strikebreakers, from running public services! We must prevent shops from opening! We must prevent traffic on the streets! We must prevent every move by the dictatorship! . . . We honor the people! Strike! Strike! Strike!"

On hearing the announcement Félix jumped into his green Volkswagen Bug and raced to an office where comrades were cranking out leaflets with the radio slogans. "Come on!" Félix exclaimed as he grabbed some leaflets and went running outside with five comrades in tow. "Get the leaflets around!" he ordered. "Throw them in the streets if you have to!"

One comrade came running back. "What kind of a general strike is this? Everything is open!"

What kind of a general strike indeed. At the moment of the broadcast, July 26th forces were attacking a private gun shop in Old Havana, trying to steal weapons. Police in the neighborhood easily stopped the robbery attempt. Fidel Castro was behind all the trouble; Félix and his fellow communists were almost alone in knowing it.

Castro and his partisans must have been spellbound by those mass eruptions that had sprung to life in Santiago de Cuba as out of thin air; they figured that if they only said the word in Havana,

Cuba's first city would go the same way.

At the eleventh hour Fidel had told his organizers to join with other groups. A few overtures went out to the communists, who grabbed at them. But finally the July 26th people in the capital had decided to act on their own.

They took almost no one into their confidence. They followed no strategy to gain support from students, workers or other key groups. They left their public announcement for the last minute. The broadcast came in the middle of a working day, giving people almost no chance to join. To top it off, the announcers gave no clue as to who they might be. Listeners had scant reason to believe them.

Assessing the event afterward, Félix thought: *Holy cow! Those people from the July 26th are as hapless as the Directorio!*

The abject failure of the strike dealt a major blow to Fidel's prestige. It also made clear that the July 26th campaign, despite some success in the provinces and a rave review in *The New York Times,* was not yet ready to bring its show to town. What it sorely lacked, and desperately needed, was the mobilizing skill and mastery of issues that the Communist Party could supply.

Angrily Fidel disavowed his own partisans. Quietly and seriously he began to deal with the communists, who could help him with organizing workers and the urban poor.

"The Party has decided that objective conditions are now favorable for supporting armed struggle against the Batista puppet regime," the general secretary of Félix's Socialist Youth cell explained to cell members.

"What does that mean about the Party's decision last year not to support the armed struggle?" César Gómez asked in a spirit of playing with the other man.

"The Party's decision to support the insurgency at this time is a demonstration that the earlier line was also correct," the general secretary said like a party-line sap.

"Really?" César wondered. "How is that?"

"Last year conditions for joining the insurgency were poor. Therefore the Party was against it. Now the Party is able to join under conditions that are much more favorable politically. Both lines are therefore correct."

César would not waste his breath on that.

Batista was riding high. A year earlier he had beaten off the Directorio because, unlike his predecessor, he knew how to keep safe in a fortress with a loyal garrison. He also knew that if the rebellion had nothing more to present than a poorly-scripted general strike, he was good for the long term.

In the short term, Batista ordered his army to attack the guerrilla movement on its home turf of Oriente province and finish it.

A year and a half earlier, Castro had landed his skeletal force in Oriente with the idea to replay his own Moncada attack and get it right this time. What might have been different in the replay? We'll never know, because the July 26th campaign did not succeed with classic military tactics or even with *guerrilla* tactics. It succeeded on a playing field that allowed Castro's unique talent to shine. That was the field of images and appearances on which victorious political movements are based.

In the mountains of eastern Cuba Fidel met the discontents of the rural people and figured out how to use those discontents for his purposes. When in May 1958 Batista launched his military offensive, the *campesinos* threw their weight behind Castro's tiny force as a protest against Batista. All at once Castro's command had legions of sympathizers giving information on the army's every move. With thousands of eyes working for the rebel force, Castro's men could strike when and where they chose.

The Rebel Army won a string of victories and took prisoners by the hundreds. Those prisoners – whom Castro could not have held in any case – were turned over to the Red Cross with not a single one mistreated. The public-relations display made for an eloquent contrast to Batista's methods.

Cuban army regulars, like soldiers everywhere, disliked having to fight against their own people. The campaign disheartened regular troops as well as their officers. Enlisted men were loath to obey orders which their officers were loath to give. The army's command structure broke down. In front of an amazed public, Batista withdrew his routed, panicked forces from eastern Cuba.

Throughout the vast eastern province of Oriente, Castro's command began quickly to work as a de facto government. In August Fidel appointed *comandante* Pastora Núñez "to visit all the proprietors of sugar plantations in Oriente Province to inform that, by military decrees of the Rebel Army, a contribution has been set of 15 centavos for each 250 lb. sack of sugar produced by the 1958 harvest . . . [Payment entitles the contributor] to the guarantees that only the Rebel Army can offer to the cane fields and to the industrial installations of all the mills of the province. Failure to comply with this in the time and form indicated will lead to sanctions that will be irrevocable as of this date."

In other words: If payments are not made, your cane fields will be burned and your machinery destroyed.

Comandante Pastora – or Pastorita, as many called her – was a woman the likes of whom the mill-owners, many of them American, probably had not met before. To the sugar planters Pastorita gave a simple choice: Yes or yes?[15] To back her up, Fidel's brother Raúl ordered the kidnapping and quick release of several Americans – a move that showed *guerrilla* resolve without giving the US grounds to retaliate. It was a perfect squeeze, and

---

[15] The phrase was shared with the author in 1992 by Pastorita's old comrade Emi Rivero.

American companies were quickly filling the coffers of Castro's regime.

Those payments coincided with a written recommendation by the US embassy: that the State Department "adhere to a policy of strict neutrality" in the fight between Batista and the rebels.[16]

That policy had been some time in coming. Ambassador Smith had had little taste for Batista or his methods.[17] And now, with American companies in Oriente paying protection money to the rebel side, official Washington was getting behind the idea that Batista must go.[18]

---

[16] https://history.state.gov/historicaldocuments/frus1958-60v06/d121

[17] For Ambassador Smith's statement in Santiago de Cuba see Chapter 6, "Self-sufficient," above; also, https://history.state.gov/historicaldocuments/frus1958-60v06/d189

[18] Ibid. On December 23 Secretary of State Christian Herter informed President Eisenhower that the State Department was working against Batista in favor of "a government broadly based on popular consent and support."

08

Takeover

Autumn 1958. The rebellion was running forward quicker than anyone could believe. As rebel armies continued to make gains, Cuba's economy, for the first time since Batista's seizure of power, fully reflected the turmoil.

A fact largely unnoted had been the robust advance of Cuba's economy even under the hated regime. But as collapse approached, uncertainty went sky-high and investment went through the floor.

Repression was tougher and more frightening than ever. It fell hardest in the cities. For every slain comrade that Fidel mourned in the Sierra Maestra, a dozen or more youngsters died in Havana police stations.

Félix's father had come to the end of his rope. The old man, whose face had crumpled in grief when he sent his favorite son away to the US, now put his foot down.

"If you are going to live here, then live here," he told his younger boy. "But if you are using this place as a communist hideout I can't allow that. It's too dangerous, I won't subject your mother to it, and I have to ask you to move somewhere else."

Adolfo betook himself to the house of a communist friend, lodging there until *el viejo* broke down and told him: "Look, whatever the consequences, your mother and I would rather have you at home."

On New Year's Eve a discouraging piece of news reached the president from central Cuba. Santa Clara, the hub of the island's rail, transport and communication networks, was facing a rebel assault and the army had gone AWOL. Divisions were scattering; commanders wouldn't come to the phone. At 10 p.m. Batista called a meeting of his loyal partisans at Havana's Columbia army barracks to bid farewell to 1958.

For most in the capital it was another New Year's Eve. Félix stayed at home and went to bed early.

"Wake up, son." It was the old man coming into his bedroom some time after midnight. "Batista is gone."

"Gone! What do you mean?"

"Gone from Cuba."

"I don't believe it," Félix said.

"It's true. He took his friends in a plane and a pile of cash in another plane."

"The old son of a whore! Where did he go?"

"To Santo Domingo, it seems.[19] He left a *junta* under Cantillo in his place." General Eulogio Cantillo had directed the previous summer's failed campaign against the Rebel Army.

"Good! That *junta* should last about five minutes."

"I give it ten," the old man said with a shrug and went to the kitchen to make coffee.

Félix hurried to phone his Party contact, Otto Vilches. "Otto! Did you hear?"

"Of course! We're still informing the Party leadership. You'd better move."

---

[19] This turned out to be accurate.

Félix put down the phone in a fever of excitement. His father gave him a coffee. The old man was taking the news like business as usual: a leader going out, a leader coming in, another crank of history's revolving door. Félix was tasting history for the first time – a taste as strong and sweet as the early morning brew that flowed over his tongue.

The lad jumped into his green Volkswagen Bug and steered it toward the center of action. At first the streets were mostly deserted but soon groups of people were riding around in trucks, calling out to each other, *"¡Viva Cuba libre!"*

How quickly the capital had fallen. Without a fight, without even a word, the old order had packed up and gone. Who would have guessed how easy it would be? On the streets, a carnival had materialized from out of a void.

Félix and his comrades had much to do. Everyone supported the rebels; no one doubted the *junta* would have to step down. But the moment was full of danger. From the other end of the island Fidel broadcast an urgent appeal to the people of Cuba, asking everyone to stay calm and raise no violence.

As the hours passed, gigantic events transpired. Officers of the regular army transferred command of Havana's key fortresses to Castro's main commanders; while in the name of the revolution, a squad of fighters from the old student Directorio seized the Presidential Palace which that group had failed to conquer less than two years before. Twenty-four hours after Batista's flight, the rebels controlled Havana.

The only people to be alarmed, a far-from-negligible group, were those who had served Batista. *Esbirros* or henchmen – Cubans called them all by that name whether they were beat cops, army colonels or presidential ministers. Since the hour of victory, rebel soldiers (or people claiming to be rebel soldiers) had been looking for *esbirros* and summarily shooting them. Havana's police had taken off their uniforms and gone into hiding.

At the main TV station Félix and his group demanded to go on air with a statement from the Socialist Youth. Without delay Félix was before the cameras and a moderator announcing: "This is a democratic, open TV station where even communists can speak."[20]

Afterward Félix realized he hadn't been home in several days. He was wrung out from exhaustion, in need of a bath and shave, so home he went.

"We haven't seen you in four days and not a phone call!" *la vieja* told him.

The boy regarded her sullenly. *We made a revolution and I still have to hear that shit.*

His dad did not quite understand. Riverito's friends in Batista's cabinet had vanished overnight. Still – or so el viejo seemed to think – he had served a quarter-century at the Presidential Palace and he knew how to befriend people.

"Look, *viejo*," Félix said. "It's not the same old thing any more. These July 26th people – you don't know them. Hell, I don't know them. I only know things will be different."

El viejo shook his head. It was beyond his reckoning that he might not make his way. As for revolutions, he'd been watching them since before the kid had been born.

---

[20] Cubans used the terms 'socialist' and 'communist' interchangeably; see note 13 in Chapter 6, "Self-sufficient," above.

09

Juggernaut

In their first weeks of power, Cuba's new rulers pushed out measures that bought them immense popularity. Urban rents were cut in half; land values lowered; vacant lots placed on sale for low-cost housing projects; utility and telephone rates slashed. To peasants in Pinar del Río, Cuba's westernmost province, Fidel himself was signing over parcels of state-owned land.

Those measures piqued the Americans who disliked anything that smacked of socialization. Especially offended were the *yanquis* who owned Cuba's telephone and utility companies, and quite a number more who owned agricultural enterprises or landed estates.

The new regime's policies also targeted Cuba's moneyed classes who had been able to save on taxes by bribing Batista's officials. Last but not least, the *esbirros* – people who had worked for Batista in any capacity – faced a triple threat. Those who were arrested got jail if they were lucky and the firing wall if they were not. All properties belonging to *esbirros*, without exception, were seized.

To the ordinary rich Cubans who owed back taxes, revenue agents offered favorable repayment terms. Most people found repayment a better option than others on offer. With back-tax payments flooding into government offices, plus proceeds from confiscated properties, Fidel's regime acquired a fortune and became the best-endowed revolution of modern times.

La chusma, the untamed mass, identified ever more strongly with the revolutionary regime. How come? Emi and his pals looked sideways at those who had done nothing against Batista's regime while saying they hated it.

To those who actually did fight against Batista, the emotional outpouring of the masses for Fidel was a blatant hypocrisy. The so-called revolutionary crowd was trying to erase its earlier inaction by giving Fidel those wild displays of support. And Fidel was happy to accept the acclaim.

Even the old fighters, with all their seriousness, did not miss out on the fun of those early days. Emi was an attorney with revolutionary credentials and good contacts in the new regime. The country's laws were in a state of total flux, while people's pockets were bulging with money from all the economic breaks the regime had given. As a lawyer Emi had never been busier, nor had he prospered more.

The honeymoon was short. Barely two months into the takeover, a group of 40-odd fighter pilots from Batista's air force went on trial for war crimes. Accused of bombing rebel positions during the recent conflict, the airmen defended themselves by saying they had actually dropped their bombs on empty areas and made false reports to their superiors. Their stories were verified, and in a surprise verdict the judge found the airmen not guilty.

Revolutionary regimes, however, tend to reject surprises which are not of their own making. That verdict enraged the revolutionary mob. A riot broke out in Santiago de Cuba, where the court had met. Across the island in Havana, Fidel went on TV and demanded a new trial. The trial judge was replaced by a *comandante*, "Redbeard,"[21] who was one of Raúl's loyal men.

Redbeard convened a second trial. On the same evidence, he convicted all the airmen and gave them prison terms of up to 30 years. Fidel pronounced a new legal standard: "Revolutionary justice is based not on legal precepts but on moral conviction . . . Since the airmen belonged to the air force of [Batista] they are criminals and must be punished."

---

[21] Manuel Piñeiro Losada, one of the regime's top intelligence officials; see also Chapter 35, "A passable evening," below.

§§§

That pronouncement had a strong clue about the nature of Fidel's regime. In their talk after Batista's overthrow, *el viejo* the savvy older man had gotten it wrong while Adolfo the greenhorn youngster had called it perfectly right.[22]

One of the regime's first edicts was to cancel the system of *botellas* or sinecures on which Riverito and other journalists depended for their livelihoods. At the same time, negative statements began appearing about journals that had prospered during Batista's rule. People who wrote for those journals – the gamut of Cuba's free press – were being called "traitors," "pharisees," "sellouts" or *"botelleros,"* which had suddenly acquired a sinister new meaning.[23]

The inference was false. Cuban newspapers heavily depended on sinecures to help them balance their accounts. Salaries were kept low in expectation that reporters – like workers in the service trades – would make much of their living in extras. The *botellas* had no relation to what anyone wrote; only to his or her standing in the profession. They were not bribes, any more than tips to your favorite waiter or concierge would be.

Of course the new rulers knew it perfectly well. They simply wouldn't miss a chance to help themselves and their friends at the expense of wealthy people from the old regime. That they did, adding insult to injury, with the holier-than-thou attitude which revolutionaries have eternally deployed against an old regime's corruption. Old-style enrichments are painted as morally bankrupt, while the new regime's money-grabs are extolled as a vital means to distribute well-being or deliver "social justice."

In short order the new rulers had Cubans accepting that the Havana newspapers of the old regime had sold their souls for

---

[22] See the last paragraphs of Chapter 8, "Takeover," just above.
[23] The young men or boys who carried *botellas* or water-bottles on the *jai alai* court were also called *"botelleros."*

sinecures. After canceling the sinecures, the new regime seized
the presses, offices and physical plants of all newspapers that had
given support to Batista. In that removal of property, officials
made no exception for journals which had shown balance by also
giving generous coverage to the rebels.[24]

The real objective was twofold: to abolish those newspapers which
the regime did not fully trust; and to enrich others – like the July
26th newspaper *Revolución* and the Communist newspaper *Hoy* –
on which the regime felt it could count 100 percent.

It was indeed a dramatic and visionary solution to the problem
of an unrestrained press. Cuban media had been free and feisty
to the point of rambunctiousness. Batista had suspended press
freedoms from time to time and been battered for it. But Batista
never imagined the 'final solution' which the new rulers now took
care to apply by stages. In the end Fidel's regime did not precisely
banish corruption. It made corruption invisible, and therefore
total, by canceling journalism itself.

Against this juggernaut, even Riverito – a man who had defended
his family through the worst of times – was no match.

In an abrupt role-change the younger son intervened on his

---

[24] "Batista and the political elite . . . even allowed the publication of twenty-five
attacks against them by Fidel Castro in the Cuban press. The nine statements
published – mostly in daily newspapers with wide circulation – either before
Castro's attack on the Moncada military barracks in July 1953 or in 1955, after
he had been released from prison and remained in Cuba thanks to Batista's
political amnesty, do not pose so much of a question. But the Cuban press
was also allowed to publish thirteen statements when Castro was already a
political exile dedicated to the violent overthrow of the Batista regime, and
two major revolutionary documentes, in 1957 and 1958, while Castro was in
the mountains fighting Batista. Castro's interview with Herbert Matthews for
The New York Times was also published in *Bohemia*, the leading Cuban news
magazine, as were sixteen of Castro's twenty-five anti-Batista statements."
Jorge I. Domínguez, *Cuba: Order and Revolution* (Harvard University Press,
1978), p. 124

father's behalf. With the revolution's coming to power the 23-year-old had gained a senior position in the Communist Party; no less a personage than Raúl Castro had appointed him to the leadership of the Party's youth organizations in the Havana district.

In Adolfo's eyes – he had put away his underground name – *el viejo* was a political innocent. He might not understand the revolution, he might not go for communism, but those were no reasons to treat him harshly. Adolfo wrote a brief in which he decorously testified that Riverito had given refuge to communist militants being hunted by Batista's police; in other words, to several of Félix's buddies who had stayed as guests in his father's house while they were on the lam.

Here was the rub: Adolfo could only give his memo to communist leaders who were still sitting in the peanut gallery. The July 26th people were the ones in power. They had no reason to help an older journalist with close ties to the *ancien régime*.

To Adolfo's parents, only one thing was certain: this was not their Cuba any more.

10

'Dammit, sir, this is communism!'

Havana, July 1959. Six months into the new regime, Emi Rivero was at his government law practice when fellow attorney Efrén Rodríguez came bursting into his office. Efrén's handsome features, which gave him a Clark Gable look, were twisted in rage and colored like a beet. Efrén chucked his briefcase onto a chair and exclaimed as a Clark Gable character might: "Dammit, sir, this is communism!"

Though he didn't know Efrén well, Emi understood the complaint perfectly. Fidel himself had promised that the bywords of the new regime would be democracy and constitutional rule.[25] But now it seemed that Cuba was getting collectivism and one-man rule.

Emi was already in contact with veterans from the anti-Batista war who talked in low voices about taking up arms again. Emi had also encountered Efrén in the anti-Batista ranks, but the man was not a close acquaintance. For all Emi knew, Efrén might be part of the regime, working as a double agent. So Emi played safe and answered with a feint.

"Look Efrén, maybe Fidel is fooling around with the *yanquis.* Maybe he's using the communists as a stalking horse to get concessions or win respect. When the revolution is secure, Fidel will have no more use for the communists and he'll be able to push them out. The communists might not be as entrenched as they seem."

---

[25] The phrase, as quoted by *The New York Times*, was: "a democratic Cuba and an end to the dictatorship." See "Cuban Rebel Is Visited in Hideout," February 24, 1957, p. 1 & ff.

"Good points," Efrén replied. "But they don't disprove what I said. Whatever he thinks he's doing, the son of a whore is selling the revolution to Moscow. He's betraying all of us!"

Emi shared those fears and badly hoped they were unfounded. He had started a new family and was making a happy life. If the *res publica* was going out of joint, he would be pulled into the battle and his sweet new life would be crossed.

He also had his parents to consider. He did not want to burden them with depressing stories at a time of their own suffering. By the summer of 1959 Riverito had lost his place in the world. And something worse: his favorite son, still living at home, had become a constant affliction.

Ever since the old ones had been together, *la vieja* had been the one to say: Let's move, let's find a new apartment, let's build a new house. Now she decided they should move to America.

Why not go for six months or a year and wait for a change? Many acquaintances were leaving for the States. Delia was sure that the two of them, even without knowing English, would be safer and more welcome there than at home. They could come back when time had softened things, as in Cuba time always did.

La vieja put their belongings up for sale and placed their luxury home on the rental market. Then Emi got another jolt: a phone call from his mother, who was not one to raise alarms.

"I need you here," she told him. "I'm having trouble with your father and your brother."

"Trouble! How so?"

"We have to sell the Volkswagen car." It was the green Bug which Adolfo had all but turned into an honorary member of the Communist Party.

"I know," Emi said sympathetically.

"Your brother is in an extremely bad mood about it."

"Okay, he's in a bad mood. What else is new?"

"Adolfito's behavior is disturbing. Your father is afraid to go near him."

"Afraid to go near him!"

"It isn't like Rivers. He is actually frightened by your brother."

She only called her husband 'Rivers' when she was tense to the point of correctness.

"Tell me what to do," Emi said.

"Come and take the car away."

"Are the papers in the glove compartment? We need them for any sale."

"Don't worry about the papers. I just need the car out of here."

Emi grabbed a taxi for the ride to the deluxe neighborhood of Miramar, sweating all the way.

The family was cracking apart. How could it be? No matter how or where they lived – and they had lived in many places – the four of them had always been a unit, as safe and secure as an old stone bridge. True, the old ones had their favorites; Emi had been his mother's special preoccupation, while the old man's love for his younger boy was operatic. But those gradations had only made the structure more solid and reliable. No matter the storms that raged against it, the old stone bridge would still be there, bright and resplendent when the sun came back. How many hurricanes had it seen and calmly forgotten?

Now things were different. At the house, Emi hardly registered who said what to whom. He only took the car keys from his mother and drove the Volkswagen away.

Thirty-plus years later, sitting in his brother's apartment, Emi poured out his anguished memories of that day while Adolfo shrugged and said he didn't remember a thing.[26]

---

[26] Emi & Adolfo Rivero in conversation with the author, Miami, 1992

11

Outside the revolution

In the summer of 1959 all but one of the Rivero family left
Havana for foreign parts.

Adolfo was the first to go. Having served as the Communist
Party's youth leader for the Havana district, he was now being
sent to Budapest as Cuba's representative to the World Federation
of Democratic Youth.

Adolfo's assignment came at a moment of extraordinary tension.
Emi's statements to his fellow lawyer Efrén, which he had spoken
as a ruse, also carried a measure of truth: Fidel was said to be
preparing a major blow against the Communists. Party leaders
put stock in the rumors; Adolfo had the impression that the Party
was sending him abroad to protect him.[27]

Not long afterward Emi took his parents to the Rancho Boyeros
Airport[28] for a very different kind of departure. *Los viejos* were
dressed in their finest for a voyage that combined glamour and
desperation. They were running from a new order that had all but
expelled them; their destination was Washington DC, where an
old friend was waiting for them. Esther Guzmán or "Tatica" was
an attorney and long-time resident of the US capital. A few years
earlier, Tatica had watched over Adolfo during his one-year stay at
Georgetown. Who could have guessed that she would be receiving
Adolfo's parents a few years hence?

---

[27] For Emi's statements see Chapter 10, "'Dammit, sir, this is communism!'"
just above. Adolfo stated his recollection about the Party leaders in our 1992
Miami interview, op cit.

[28] Now José Martí International Airport

Emi remained in Havana with his family, which now included
a new son and daughter: two-going-on-three-year-old Rubén
and one-going-on-eleven-year-old "Ermi" – her own rendering
of 'Irma' which her father, with his love of nicknames, quickly
adopted.

Emi had joined the ranks of happy, humdrum men who are
invisible to the chronicle of turmoil known as history. And it was
easy to believe him when he said that for the sake of his family he
would rather have stayed away from history's spotlight. But with
his character and in the temper of the time, staying away was not
really a choice.

In October 1959 an ominous sequence began to unfold when
comandante Huber Matos, the liberator of Santiago and one
of the Rebel Army's most popular officers, resigned his post as
military chief of Camagüey province. Matos published an open
letter to Fidel expressing sadness at the prevalence of communists
in official positions. He said he must in conscience remove
himself while pledging personal support to the revolution's leader.

Matos might have been stating his views with an extra gentleness
because he wanted to keep alive politically. But his demure tone
did not keep Fidel from acting quickly and forcefully. The leader
ordered *comandante* Camilo Cienfuegos to travel to Camagüey
and place Matos under arrest. When Camilo arrived, Matos
warned his younger comrade to take care for his own life. Matos
then gave himself up and went to Havana in custody.

A little more than a week later, the plane returning Camilo from
Camagüey to Havana was lost at sea. A massive search for the
plane was said to yield nothing.

Meanwhile, the man in charge of the Camagüey control tower
was an apparent suicide; while at the Columbia army barracks
in Havana Captain Cristino Naranjo, a favorite officer of
Camilo's who had openly questioned the official version of the
disappearance, was machine-gunned to death in a supposed
accident.

Those three deaths have never been solved. But Emi and others who had fought against Batista were not in doubt. Camilo was the most popular and beloved of the revolution's *comandantes*. Fidel's displeasure at the prolonged ovations given to Camilo at mass rallies was plainly visible to TV viewers. And now Camilo was conveniently gone, along with two possible witnesses. The best explanation seemed to be the obvious one.

From that moment on, Emi and his buddies counted themselves 'outside the revolution.' When a revolution killed its enemies, it was hard but understandable. When a revolution killed its friends it went beyond redemption.

12

Cavaradossi

At the end of 1959 Emi went to Washington DC to look in on his parents. They had left Tatica's place for a small flat in the DC suburb of Arlington, Virginia.

El viejo had taken work as a busboy in a Washington hotel. He earned an immigrant's wage, and the work was grueling. When a rough supervisor told him to work harder, *el viejo* gathered up his meager English and said: "You kill people, but you aren't going to kill me."

Living in America had turned *el viejo* into a boy all over again. When he left the hotel one evening, he found that a fresh coat of snow had fallen on the city; his markers were buried, and he completely lost his way.

The night that Emi stayed with his parents, the old man emptied his pockets to bring home a bottle of red wine – a kindness that would live as starkly in the son's mind as events that were soon to reshape his life.

As much as he had lost and suffered, Riverito thought first of his boys. But "home" was home no more, and Adolfo was in another world thousands of miles away.

In Budapest with the World Federation of Democratic Youth,[29] Adolfo was the senior Cuban in Hungary and Cuba's *de facto* ambassador. As an envoy of Cuba's new order Adolfo traveled the length and breadth of the continent, giving impassioned talks to rapt audiences and bringing them to tears over the miracle of the revolution.

In private he complained about having to twiddle his thumbs as an international bureaucrat while at home the revolution was pushing forward. But in Adolfo's case 'home' was something more than the revolution. It was the big, fat problem he had left behind: his family.

Before Emi's Washington visit Adolfo had written his parents: "Separated as you are from all you love, I can't imagine that you're happy or will be happy. I didn't agree with your leaving, as you'll remember. But let's hope the hard times don't get you down. . . ."

Adolfo didn't hesitate to lecture his parents about politics. As he wrote his father in November 1959: "Your work allowed you to get ahead in life and you came to believe that in our society the man who works can advance himself. But it's not true. You worked a lot but plenty of people worked a lot harder and never got anywhere at all, they never enjoyed anything . . .

"The revolution is preparing a new life where there will be work and a future for all Cubans. It's clear that the revolution – in the course of cleaning up and changing the whole system of corruption, of treason, of dirty politics, of handing our national treasure to the *yanquis* and all the other evils we know about – will inevitably visit harm on people who had no role in those past miseries. It's also clear that as the revolution secures itself, things

---

[29] This group was part of a Europe-wide youth movement with Soviet sympathies. At the height of their activity during the Cold War, the Federation and its associated groups were underwritten by entities of the Soviet Bloc and were duly infiltrated by Western intelligence agencies. After 1989 the World Federation made a place for itself in the post-communist world.

will 'take their level' – not their old level but their new level, a new life for the Cuban people – a life without so much bitterness, without so much suffering, with instead a great concern for all mankind, a life more humane and worthwhile which is what we're fighting for. In that new life we will have room for everybody . . ."

In another letter to his father, Adolfo wrote: "Emi has started a bourgeois house and carries on with the grey, boring routine of his petty individualism . . . I'll tell you plainly how proud I am to see you on your feet, ready to work, no matter how humble and exhausting the work may be . . . The important thing is the solidarity, the spiritual closeness that exists between us, and which does not exist between Emi and me."

Emi, for his part, disliked turning on the revolution and liked even less the idea of turning on his brother. But nature was pressing him to oppose the very things Adolfo revered: the Party, the leader, the unitary state. Like Mario Cavaradossi, the hero of his favorite opera *Tosca*, Emi felt his ideals pushing him into the fight. So he put aside his druthers and went toward it.

On a beautiful December morning Emi paid a visit to the FBI building and got on a guided tour. At the end of the tour he did not exit with other visitors but waited for someone to ask why he was still there. To the guard who approached him, Emi said in his impeccable English that he would like to speak with an official. He was shown to a cubicle and invited to sit down.

When the official came in, Emi gave his name and took note of the other man's. He waited for the prompt and said tersely: "I'm a Cuban visiting in Washington. And I've come to see you because I'm concerned about what's going on in my country."

"Then perhaps you want to see the CIA," the other man kindly noted. "The FBI doesn't get involved in matters outside the United States."

"Thank you, sir. I know that what you say is now true. But it hasn't always been. My family was close to the center of Cuban politics for many years. My father, who now lives in Arlington, used to be a journalist at Cuba's Presidential Palace. He often had praise for the Bureau's agents who were detailed to Havana. So for me this visit to the FBI is a kind of tribute. I feel honored to be here. I didn't come to say anything specific. And I will not take more of your time. I only wanted to tell you I'm concerned."

With an operatic gesture all his own, Emi rose to his feet and left.

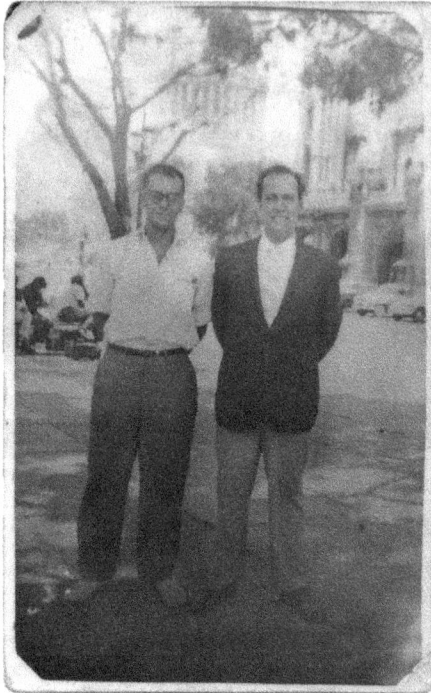

May 10, 1960: a breaking point

13

Civil war

Havana, May 1960. Emi got a call from his parents. They were frantic with concern about Adolfo. He had promised to stop over and see them on a visit from Budapest to Cuba; but since receiving that promise they had neither seen nor heard from him. They didn't know whether he was in Cuba, Hungary, or Siberia. They implored Emi to locate his brother and get news of him.

Like his father Emi was no mean detective. He convinced his enemies, the communists, to disclose Adolfo's whereabouts.

Adolfo was indeed in Havana at a congress of his home organization, which was now called the Rebel Youth. Emi also managed to ferret out Adolfo's sleeping quarters: the Deauville, a rather swish hotel along Havana's seaside boulevard or *Malecón*. Emi got hold of Adolfo and invited him to lunch.

Adolfo was a willing participant but by no means a congenial one. When they met at the Havana Reporters' Association, itself a death-bound entity, Adolfo began with the words, *"Estás sobrealimentado"* – You're overfed.

They walked toward the Chinese restaurant Cantón. As meetings between them had become extremely rare, they stopped to have a Polaroid taken by a street photographer. Surely this commission was a nostalgic tribute to *el viejo* who had begun his phenomenal rise to prominence by snapping portraits of tourists in Havana's cafés.

In this portrait Adolfo looks the part of the well-to-do tourist that he is – a visitor from Budapest, all smiles, with a boyish nonchalance. Emi produces a smile of sorts but it's an obvious push; the down-turned corners of his eyes and mouth betray that the meeting is no picnic for him, either.

At the restaurant they went straight to business. Adolfo mentioned the low-cost housing project being organized by *comandante* Pastora Núñez. Enemies of the government had criticized her for ignoring legal procedures in efforts to speed up construction.

"The important thing is to build the houses," Adolfo said. "The rest of it can be dealt with in its proper time."

"I agree," Emi said. "It's a good project and needs to be done quickly."

"How about the other revolutionary measures?" Adolfo asked. "Where do you stand on those?"

'Revolutionary measures' was a candy-coated term for confiscations of wealth that the regime had visited on many Cubans and Americans.

"Governments have a right to take properties," Emi answered, stating the matter without euphemisms. "It's part of the political contract. I don't object to that."

Ever the interrogator, Adolfo pressed in. "Do you accept the leadership of Fidel Castro?"

"I don't accept the leadership of anyone," Emi said firmly.

"Fidel is pushing things in the right direction. The country accepts him and so should you."

"Like everyone else? I don't think so."

"Then you're not being smart about it. You wanted the revolution as much as anyone. It's *your* revolution too. Why not find your place in it? But no, that would make you like other people. So you do the contrary and screw up your life!"

"I won't work with communists. Look Adolfito, it's nothing to do with you. If you had become a priest I wouldn't have liked it, but as you're my brother I would have wanted you to become the Pope. I don't like your being a communist but since you are one, I want you to reach the highest positions in the Party hierarchy. I want you to succeed."[30]

"But I don't want you to succeed!"

"Listen. *Los viejos* are suffering because of their separation from us. Call them once in a while, would you? Even if the Party is

---

[30] This statement is quoted by journalist Dora Amador in her news-breaking article about the Rivero brothers: «Dos hermanos», *el Nuevo Herald*, Miami, January 28, 1990.

paying your expenses, they must understand you have to talk with your parents."

"Don't compare your morals with mine," Adolfo said roughly.

Lunch was over with an abrazo; they were still brothers, after all. As they hugged, Emi could feel a lot of things in Adolfo's musculature: the wiriness of a zealot, the buzzing excitement of revolutionary power, the staunchness of the man's principles, a leanness that came from self-denial, and a warmth which Emi felt to be a strong love for *los viejos*.

But sentiments made little difference in the oncoming conflict. Cubans were quickly taking sides. Armed groups of veterans from Fidel's own Rebel Army had started forming units in the countryside, preparing to do to Fidel what Fidel had done to Batista. Emi was already working with one of those groups.

Adolfo, who soon returned to Budapest and without stopping in Washington, likewise knew a bridge had been crossed. Counting the days until he could go home for good, Adolfo busied himself with thoughts of Emi's likely activity. The contact with his folks that Adolfo had suspended now looked useful to him. In letters from Budapest he flooded his parents with warnings for his brother.

"Tell Emi this is not like the fight against Batista. Castro is much more capable and his popularity is overwhelming. If Emi tries to conspire now, he will not make more of his miraculous escapes. Almost certainly he will be captured and killed."

In another message: "You must tell Emi not to be so foolish as to play the trumpet in Louis Armstrong's house." In yet another, with finality: "Can it be that my brother's ambition will lead him down the path of treason?"

Emi mulled over his brother's advice. "Find yourself a place in the revolution!" It was vintage Adolfo, blunt and cogent. All it needed was the right orientation. Emi's place in the revolution would be against it – and against his brother too.

14

Resignation

Havana. "El Moro," the Moor, was one of Emi's trusted comrades. A strapping Lebanese who bubbled with humor, he was by day an inspector for the Havana bus system and at all times the most reliable of conspirators.

Toward the end of May 1960 the Moor paid Emi a visit. "*Doctor,* I have a message from Plinio," he said. "You have to go and see him as soon as possible."

"Okay," Emi told the Moor, "I'm leaving immediately."

After a seven-hour drive to the sanatorium town of Topes de Collantes, and then a climb of several hours through overgrown mountainous terrain which he had to clear with a machete, Emi was in an encampment of men who looked very much like the poster images of Castro's *guerrilla* heroes.

Plinio Prieto, a *comandante* in the anti-Batista war and now a comrade in the anti-Castro resistance, had set up a *guerrilla* hideout in the Sierra del Escambray, a mountain range in the center of the island. Emi esteemed Plinio highly. Unlike other Cuban fighters, he was cool and methodical. He didn't exaggerate, he was undemonstrative, and emotions did not color his judgments. His courage was the opposite of bravado. Some called Plinio "cold," perhaps because his very calmness made them shiver; but in Victor Hugo's phrase he was hot as fire and cold as ice at the same time.

"Our base is developing," Plinio told Emi in front of his men. "People are helping us. Many feel betrayed by the revolution. Kids who joined the Rebel Army and went to Havana are coming back with complaints about communist indoctrination and anti-American propaganda. We have men ready to fight. We just don't have weapons."

On taking power, Fidel had ordered that all who fought against Batista must surrender their arms to the new regime. "Why should any of us have guns?" he had said in his inaugural talk, pushing out the phrase three times. "*¿Armas para qué? ¿Armas para qué? ¿Armas para qué?*"

Across the island, men and women of every faction complied – and when they had done so, Fidel's troops were the only force in Cuba with guns. Anyone else who wanted to start a fight must build up a new supply of arms, which was no easy task.

"We have some guns in Havana," Emi said, "but only the ones people kept as mementos – not nearly enough to equip a fighting force."

"Then you have to go abroad, and right away. We need arms for 150 men and we can't lose time. Carry your short-wave radio. Keep us posted. We'll do the same."

Back at home Emi moved quickly and carefully. He wrote cordial letters to his employers – the government regulatory commission which he served as a lawyer, and his *alma mater*, a top high school called the Vedado Institute, where he now taught English.

Both were official bodies, and Emi had to be delicate. He begged permission to take a short leave of absence in order to explore a job prospect in the United States. Even as he wrote, Cuba's customary relations with the US were slipping away. So he added a proviso in keeping with the general uncertainty. If he was gone for more than a month, he asked to be considered as having resigned.

To his wife Pelén[31] and her mother Dr. S. – the latter a colleague at Vedado Institute – he gave the same cover story, not wanting to involve them in danger.

Of course he omitted the part about resigning. No matter what the circumstance, a man didn't resign from his family. His wife and children were tethers that fastened him to the human race. Without them he was an animal.

---

[31] 'Pelén' was a nickname and a one-of-a-kind love call; Emi had picked up an exclamation from a commercial for the popular Hatuey beer and shaped it into a nickname for the woman he adored. *"¡Ave María Pelencho, qué bien me siento!"* "Hail Mary, *gosh golly*, how good I feel!" https://www.thecubanhistory.com/2014/07/cuban-characters-ave-maria-pelencho-photos-personajes-cubanos-ave-maria-pelencho-fotos/

Part Two

Wars

15

Stage names

June 1960. From his parents' flat in Arlington, Emi telephoned to the Central Intelligence Agency, where he had established a contact some time after his visit to the FBI.

"I'm the man from Cuba with whom you spoke a couple of months ago," Emi said.

"As well I remember!" the CIA man responded. "It's not every day that someone walks into our building by the front door and bellows through the lobby, 'I would like to talk about Cuba!'"

"I promised I would visit again," Emi reminded.

"I had no doubts..."

"I might be here seven days. Or I might be here seven years."

"Are you in Arlington?"

"That's a good memory."

"It's my training. Can you meet tomorrow?"

"Of course."

"Good. I'll wait for you. And bring a suitcase. We need you on this side of the river."

That was progress. They had looked into his story and found they could check the boxes.

Next day, in a Washington hotel guest room, Emi's contact introduced him to another man. "As of now this man is going to be your contact."

Emi wished it could be the man he knew, but that kind of attachment made no sense and he let it go.

"Please call me J.B.," the new man said, extending his hand.

"A pleasure to meet you," Emi said, taking the firm clasp and returning it. He liked the man's presence but felt uneasy about the *nom de guerre*; he knew the Archibald MacLeish play of that name[32] and didn't like the coincidence.

"Your English is excellent! And what am I to call you?" J.B. asked.

"Brand."

"After Ibsen's character?"

"Yes. It seems we have both taken identities from the theater."

J.B. smiled. He was a tall, slender man, well-groomed, patrician, highly educated and somehow nondescript. "You look like someone I know," Brand told him.

"Actually I look like everyone," J.B. answered.

Of course, Brand thought. *This man is the perfect agent – a face in the crowd. He knows what he's about.*

Brand gave J.B. a full account of the Cuban situation. He argued that America's best allies in the current situation were those who had earlier fought against Batista – that is, against America's ally. Aside from having the experience of that toughening fight, they were people of principle whose goals had been betrayed by

---

[32] *J.B.*, the story of Job re-told for the Broadway stage

Castro. They wanted his regime gone for the same reasons US officials did.

The American said nothing against the idea and seemed to be in sync with it. Brand took it as a cue to state a candid detail of his present situation.

"Plinio asked me to keep in contact with him via short-wave. But since then I've been unable to raise him."

"We might be able to help you there," J.B. said.

"Really!" Brand exclaimed, incredulous.

"We're also prepared to offer you a contract and an agent's salary," J.B. added, going straight to his objective and seeming to ignore Brand's disbelief.

"J.B., I came here because I'm Cuban and I'm working for Cuba. I'm prepared to work with your people in Cuba and with you here. More than anything, and urgently, I need weapons."

"The weapons will be there, Brand. Have no doubts about it. But first we need to have forces in place."

"Our people in the Escambray are already there. They will start fighting as soon as they have weapons. Plus that, we have a group forming in Pinar del Río. If we can move quickly I think we have a chance. But soon Castro will be unbeatable. I don't have to tell you time is short."

Indeed he did not. While J.B. kept his face in perfect order, Brand could sense pressure in the other man's breathing and in the curt, tense movements of his hands.

"You do your part and I'll do mine," J.B. said. "In the meantime, don't worry about funds. Whatever money you need to organize yourselves, you'll have it."

"I want political support for our group in the event we succeed."

"You'll have that too."

Here ended their first meeting as J.B. left the room. And here in this hotel Brand would remain until the CIA had further need of him.

16

Underground

Brand's first feeling had been one of progress. But as he moved his mind over J.B.'s responses, he felt on edge.

The other man's largesse with money was the first item to lose its sheen. Americans threw money at difficult situations. Rather than a commitment, it was a defense and a snare. When they gave you money, they thought they owned you. Armaments on the other hand conferred independence, and J.B.'s statements about supplying arms were hardly more than polite. The *yanquis* were withholding the guns he needed.

A phenomenal piece of news cut off this brooding. J.B. called another meeting and told Brand: "We have Plinio."

"What do you mean, you have Plinio?"

"We found out that Castro's people had raided the camp. They arrested most of the men but Plinio and some others escaped. Government forces hunted for Plinio and couldn't find him. So we went into the Escambray and found him ourselves. Since Castro's forces were looking for him all over the island, it wasn't safe for him to stay there. We felt it made sense to bring him out."

Brand paused to take it all in. "Where is he now?"

"In this area. I've already met him."

"You have!"

"He doesn't look Cuban at all. In fact he has the face of a British officer."

That was Plinio all right; J.B. had caught the grey-eyed, fair-haired man in a phrase. And what a story J.B. had told! It was a maneuver that silenced criticism.

In Washington the two Cuban comrades met frequently and kept up their work – training, thinking, strategizing, plotting for contingencies.

"Of one thing I'm convinced," Brand told J.B. "It would be a mistake to put Plinio back into Cuba right now."

"Why?"

"Plinio is a warrior, not a conspirator. When the battle is fought, no one will lead it better than he. But for now we are dealing with Castro's police and spies. Castro's best weapons are his spies. If you don't have a sixth sense about espionage, you don't get onto the battlefield with Fidel. Plinio doesn't have that sense. His hideout was raided because his group had been infiltrated. If you send Plinio into Cuba without weapons already there, the same thing will happen again. And next time he might not be so lucky."

"Don't worry about Plinio. We know what we're doing there."

That was Brand's signal to start worrying. US intelligence had gained control of Brand's operation. The effort now moved on an American timetable.

Brand did not have to read far between the lines in order to see that he and Plinio were not the ones on whom US officials were pinning their hopes. The US was favoring the Catholic-humanist Movement of Revolutionary Recovery (MRR), a group that viewed the situation in very bright colors – overly optimistic ones.

Brand was well acquainted with the MRR. He viewed them as dedicated people, worthy of respect but lacking in experience. At age 32 Brand was a veteran of the anti-Batista rebellion. So at 25 was his brother. But the Catholic-minded group had not gone into that fight. In this one they were raw recruits.

Even in his limited movements around the US capital, Brand had seen MRR agents. He guessed they were telling US officials that the MRR had infiltrated Castro's army. In Brand's view, Castro had infiltrated the MRR. Of course that didn't keep MRR people from saying what American officials wanted to hear; and it was only human for the CIA people to be eating up those reports.

J.B. said he wanted Brand back in Havana, working with US agents there. Brand would get funds for setting up contacts, organizing anti-Castro networks in the cities, finding safe houses, "drop-zones" for weapons and so on. J.B. told Brand that the US was not going to ship weapons to him via its own supply-routes. If Brand wanted those weapons, he had to make routes of his own.

As a consequence Brand spent weeks in travel between Washington, Miami and other places, looking for people and means to move arms into Cuba as soon as he got them. In the midst of his labors Brand invited his wife, Pelén, to come from Havana to Miami.

The woman was distraught. She felt like a widow whose husband is still alive. She had lost so much weight that people who knew her well, meeting her in Miami, failed to recognize her.

Brand told her: "It seems I've got a job. Pretty soon you'll have to take the kids to the embassy and get visas."

The more he said, the less she felt she knew.

The first thing she didn't know was that Emi Rivero no longer existed. Cuban authorities had a record of his leaving the country but that passport was being retired. When he returned he would be Brand – completely underground, a man with no identity in Cuban society. To let him return through a port of entry, J.B. gave him a passport that turned him into a citizen of another Latin country; he would pass through that country on his way home, and in Cuba he would give the false passport to American agents.

By August Brand had mapped out a number of possible supply routes for weapons and was ready to leave. The CIA man, always generous in his personal attentions to Brand, saw him off at the airport. As Brand boarded the plane he repeated to J.B.: "Don't send Plinio back to Cuba!" And added: "Don't kill him!"

17

Saucerman

Meeting his CIA contact in Havana, Brand decided the other man must have come to earth in a flying saucer.

What else would you say about an American officer, sprung from the stock of John Paul Jones and Nathan Hale, who not only spoke pure Cuban and had a full command of Cuban mannerisms but who in his gestures, in his gait, in the jokes he told, was more Cuban than the Cubans?

He was Saucerman.

The Americans were keeping Brand holed up in an apartment on J.B.'s orders while they checked their sources to make sure Brand's entry into Cuba had not been detected. During this seclusion Brand's only company was Saucerman, who came to see him every day with food, newspapers and magazines.

They had long talks. Brand was struck by the fact that Saucerman personally undertook many assignments he could easily have given to Cubans. Rather than play the role of a bureaucrat, Saucerman was putting his hands on the most earth-bound details. You couldn't buy devotion like that with a salary.

"The underground movement is extremely strong," Saucerman said over and over. "Castro's days are numbered."

"Let's hope you're right," Brand replied. He was torn by the assessment. A positive viewpoint would keep the Americans in the fight; but if Saucerman's optimism was any clue, his CIA superiors were reading things badly.

After a seemingly endless confinement in the flat, Brand was cleared to resume his activity. His handler gave him a set of disguises along with a .45 caliber pistol.

"Plinio is back in Havana," Saucerman told him.

Okay, that was not good, but finally Brand was on the street in Havana and ready for action, disguised from head to toe. Aside from a wig and moustache, he had put a folded newspaper page in one shoe to change his walk; he wore an upper-body girdle to throw his shoulders back; he had put an object in his mouth to alter his speech and the line of his jaw.

Passing through the El Vedado neighborhood in a taxi, he noticed a group of schoolboys on a sidewalk – among them Emilito, his son from Lizbet. In all the years since his parting from her, hardly a week had passed without his seeing the boy.

Looking out on that group of teenaged boys and seeing several familiar faces, he beat down every impulse in his body to let the taxi go on.

As quickly as he could, he gathered up the strands of his old network. He made contact with Plinio's wife Amparo – an ideal partner, combining in herself the gritty courage of a warrior with the feminine strength of a mother and wife.

Through Amparo, Brand and Plinio coordinated their searches and met constantly. Plinio worked at setting up lines of supply for his base in the Escambray. He also made contacts inside the "Rebel" Army, which had been the official army for close to two years.

Brand was suspicious of army contacts and wouldn't use them in his own work; but Plinio's effort was Plinio's and Brand would not interfere. His own frantic researches were for ways to create chaos in Havana – the second part of a two-pronged strategy.

The first, Plinio's part, was to seize a portion of territory in the countryside and raise a flag over it. Second was to make a big disruption in the country's governance and open the way for an intervention from abroad, ideally by a coalition of American states.

In Brand's view the possibilities for disruption were twofold. One was to assassinate Castro, an idea so obvious that it had become a practical impossibility. The other was to attack Communist Party headquarters. As far as Brand could tell, that idea was unique to him and he considered it promising.

18

Amateurs

(from Emi Rivero's recollections)

Many players in the anti-Castro resistance were political amateurs. Encouraged by US advice and support, they were conspiring against professional cadres directed by a guileful leader who had the full backing of the Soviet Union, a nation of enormous means in the counterintelligence field.

In that situation I met and worked with many men and women who were generously offering themselves in a cruel war against a lethal enemy. Most of those people had been recruited and encouraged by high officials of the Cuban Catholic Church, which had entered into an opportunistic partnership with the CIA.[33]

During 1960 and 1961 the leader of the Catholic resistance group MRR was Rogelio González Corzo. Known in clandestine life as "Francisco," a man in his middle or late 20's, Francisco was an extremely serious person, tireless in his efforts to build a clandestine network and full of courage at a time when danger seemed to be haunting everyone in the underground.

In early September 1960 I went to an apartment in the El Vedado district, expecting to see Francisco with whom I would coordinate plans for drop-zones and possible actions in Havana. But Francisco was not there. A physician, Dr. Andrés Cao, told me the meeting with Francisco would take place in a different part of town, half an hour distant. I could fit this change into

---

[33] See Chapter 16, "Underground," above.

my program – although, not planning on it, I had come in a taxi without bothering to use one of my regular drivers.

Dr. Cao offered to take me to the meeting in his car. When we left the apartment, I was surprised to see he had parked almost in front of the house.

"Listen, Dr. Cao. When you come to a meeting of this kind, don't you leave your car some distance from the meeting place?"

"It's not necessary. No one is watching us. You don't need to be concerned."

We had not been on our way for five minutes when Dr. Cao told me we were being tailed.

"Make a turn and we'll see," I said, controlling my anger. After several turns we had no doubts.

I said: "We need a building with two entrances. We leave the car, go into one entrance and out the other. Do you know a building like that around here?"

"Calixto García Hospital! It's a compound with many buildings."

"Good. Let's step on it."

 In 20 minutes we were at the hospital grounds. As we parked, the car following us was parking not far away. I got out and quickly walked toward one of the buildings, closely followed by Dr. Cao.

As I reached the main hall of the building I went into a corner, tore off my moustache, removed my glasses and coat, loosened my collar and tie, rolled up my shirt-sleeves and came out of the building through the same door I had entered. The whole thing took no more than 60 seconds. In walking out, I probably crossed paths with the officers following us.

Near the hospital's main gate I got a cab and reached my next meeting. My comrades there laughed at the wrath in my voice when I told them what had just happened.[34]

---

[34] Dr. Cao went into exile and started a medical practice in Miami. He remained a lifelong friend of Brand's.

19

Red menace

{from Emi Rivero's recollections}

The headquarters of the Communist Party was on Carlos III Avenue, a principal Havana boulevard. The communists were still separate from the government. In formal terms they were not even supposed to be a party, although secretly they continued to work like one.[35]

I knew the feelings of many people in the armed forces about the ascendancy of communists in official structures; about the constant training and drilling of "red brigades;" about the mass indoctrinations in the army and in society.

An attack that destroyed the main communist leaders would kindle an enthusiasm throughout the armed forces and government that Castro would find difficult to contain. It was bound to cause a sudden and violent schism in the government. I was certain enough about the importance of the attack to plan on leading it personally.

I had some weapons available to me in Havana. I considered whether I myself should carry a Thompson submachine gun or an M3. I decided on the M3, which is less accurate than the Thompson but sturdier and less prone to problems. It was going to be a close-range fight inside a building where fire volume, not accuracy, would give the advantage.

---

[35] In the name of revolutionary solidarity, the regime had declared an end to political parties; but as Adolfo and his buddies were to learn, it didn't quite work as advertised. See Chapter 26, "Revolutionary democracy," below.

The aim of the attack was to leave no one in the building alive. I didn't like to think of what would happen in case my brother should be working there at the time. The main communist leaders, however, had to be there. So I would not act without precise information about the Party offices.

In this regard I was surprised at how difficult it was for me to learn even the simplest things I needed to know. Just like Fidel, the communists were defending themselves with an aggressive counterintelligence.

And so in their way were the Americans. In early October I got a message from Saucerman. In essence it said: "Look Brand, about that action you're planning, we don't think you have the forces in place to carry it out."

That message was another surprise. The attack on Party headquarters was my project. I had not tried to get the CIA involved and had not told my American contacts about it. Neither had I tried to keep it secret from them. I had discussed it with Francisco, who worked closely with the Americans.

The CIA people were correct in their assessment. My plan was to attack as soon as I had the needed elements in place. Since I had not attacked, it was obvious I didn't feel ready. Why then did they feel the need to pass me the message? Probably to let me know I couldn't make a plan without their finding it out.

20

Not any man

On meeting Benito F., a friend who was helping with research for the attack in Havana, Brand received a piece of news he had not expected.

"We've seen your wife," Benito said. "Listen, you've got to have a visit with her. That woman is destroyed."

"Will you set it up?"

"At once."

Telling her that a friend of her husband's was waiting to see her, Benito brought Pelén to an apartment he owned. Instead of the friend, she found her husband.

Before anything, they did what nearly all young couples are wont to do on meeting after a prolonged separation.

When they had done, she asked: "Emi, what's going on? I don't understand!"

"I'm trying to get rid of this son of a bitch."

"Why can't you be with us? Why can't we see you?"

"It's too dangerous. Listen, you have to take the kids to the US embassy and get visas. I want you to move to Miami. You'll have help at the embassy, and my friends in the States will help you there. Once you're in Miami I'll be able to stay with you in a normal way."

"Emi, take care of yourself!"

Her reaction had been very caring. Whatever else was true of Pelén, she loved her husband fully; and that was too bad for her. This young woman who had it all – beauty, sweetness, manners, taste – was built to make any man happy. But the one she had chosen was Brand, a person whom life had stamped as "not any man."

21

Dilettante

{from Emi's recollections}

From time to time, US agents in Havana arranged meetings between their Cuban friends who then could help each other. One of those Cubans working with the US was a man I will call Ricardo.

Ricardo was well known in social and business circles. He had a reputation for being sophisticated, gentlemanly and discerning. He was also, if not the wealthiest man in Cuba, someone far beyond financial worry for himself or his descendants.

When I heard from the Americans that Ricardo wanted me to contact him, I was glad about it. While most of my fellow conspirators gave their attention to purely military matters, I always had some of mine directed to politics; and Ricardo, though not directly engaged in politics, could become an important political asset.

Ricardo was a man in his early or middle forties, grey-haired, well groomed, affable without being familiar, apparently ready to give his cooperation, self-confident and at the same time cautious.

I saw he was not a man to bring into the nitty-gritty of underground operations. Rather, I should consider him and his contacts as possible sources of safe houses, vehicles, drop-zones and of course information.

After exchanging some comments with Ricardo about the rise of discontent over Castro's regime, I mentioned the desirability of creating links between conspirators and businessmen, so at the time of victory we would not be strangers to each other.

I told Ricardo that a good way of starting an exchange of views would be to look for alternatives to the agrarian reform already enacted by the government. I asked him to prepare a draft project of agrarian reform that reflected his ideas and those of his friends.

The anti-government revolutionaries among whom I counted myself were strongly of the view that whatever the future might bring, the peasants were entitled to fair treatment.

Ricardo said he would consult his friends and give me an answer.

"In that case," I said, "let's meet in two weeks." I wanted him to have ample time for arranging the various logistical items I had requested, as well as making a draft for a new agrarian law, a sensitive and complex matter that required careful consideration by many parties.

At our next meeting I found him more cordial and less reticent, though still cautious. He had done some work on my requests and promised to do more. Feeling pleased with the man, I asked: "Do you have anything on the agrarian reform project?"

"Oh yes," he answered with confidence. "Here it is." Opening a drawer, he took out an envelope and handed it to me.

I was surprised at the thinness of the envelope. I had expected a bulky manila one or a folder with many pages, perhaps including graphics, statistics or things of the sort; but no, it was a single page wherein a succinct text called for the land situation in Cuba to be brought back to December 31, 1958, the last day of Batista's rule.

I was stunned. Were Ricardo and his friends completely devoid of senses? Had the mass mobilizations of the last 19 months taught them nothing? Hadn't the huge peasant crowds visiting Havana moved their thinking patterns, if not their hearts?

Did these rich *bourgeois* want to perpetuate, if we were victorious, a longing for Castro and his irresponsible dealings with Cuba's economy? Didn't Ricardo and his friends understand that we had to create alternatives which were economically viable and, above all, socially appealing?

I thanked him for the evident attention he had given to all my requests and said I would contact him soon. I never looked for him again. In my view, he and his friends were more dangerous to our cause than all of Castro's security people put together.

22

A hero's life

By late October Plinio had organized his lines of supply in
Havana, while Brand had obtained from his CIA contacts the
promise of a weapons drop in the Escambray.

Plinio was ready to leave for the new hideout, which he had never
seen and whose precise location he did not know. He was to travel
to the center of the island and meet an escort who would lead
him up to the camp.

Saying farewell in Havana, Brand embraced Plinio and said: "If
you die and I reach power, I will give a hundred thousand dollars
to your family. If I die and you reach power, you will give a
hundred thousand dollars to my family."

Plinio's wife Amparo shook her head. "Don't say that! Neither one
of you is going to die!"

Some days later, Brand was walking in Havana when he ran into
another comrade who gave occasional help to him and Plinio.
The other man pulled him aside.

"Bad news. Plinio, on his way to the hideout, was captured by
militia."

Brand went silent. Militia troops were the "armed people,"
volunteers who went where the regime directed.

After a pause the other man said: "That's not all. A weapons drop
of 13 parachutes has also been captured."

Now Brand had reason to talk to the Weird Sisters. What had
gone wrong?

According to the best information that Brand later received, Plinio and his companion, on reaching the Escambray with their radio transmitter, couldn't establish contact with their comrades who were already running from a large contingent of Rebel Army troops.

Plinio and his comrade joined up with another group of resistance fighters. They spent several days walking in the mountains with their heavy radio equipment. While sneaking across an agricultural cooperative, they encountered a squad of militia soldiers and traded fire with them.

Hiding in thick vegetation under cover of night, they tried to make radio contact with the US in order get the arms drop delayed; but their transmissions didn't get through and the plane flew that night over the occupied campsite, dropping the arms into enemy hands.

The men broke into separate groups. Plinio and another man were taken prisoner in the town of Cumanayagua.

Other information came from the man arrested with Plinio. Apparently the police had picked up the two of them on a whim. As Plinio was shown into the squad car, police noticed his feet covered with blood. The prisoners were being held in a lockup when someone came into the station and exclaimed: "Hey! Do you know who that is?"

Plinio went on trial at once, the conclusion foregone. He was so cool in the face of his destiny – or so bored with the verbal rigmarole of the court – that he fell asleep in the middle of his own trial.

Sentenced to death and waiting to be shot, Plinio saw through the grille window of his cell door that one of the arresting officers had come to look at him. The visit was a pure act of cruelty; the policeman was invading a condemned man's privacy to catch a glimpse of his unhappiness.

Seeing the policeman's face in the door, Plinio began to whistle a popular tune, *"Yo no soy monedita de oro para caerle bien a todos"* – I am not a little gold coin to make everybody happy.[36] The policeman, or so Plinio's comrade later said, was mortified.

As important as Brand's actions in Havana might be, they were not the crux of his strategy. The main action was to take a piece of ground in the center of the island, confound the government, raise confusion, give a pretext for outside forces to enter, and bring down the show.

With Plinio's destruction the plan lay in ruins. Everything must be re-thought and built up again from scratch. That undertaking was not possible in Havana. Brand had to confer directly with J.B. in Washington.

---

[36] https://www.youtube.com/watch?v=Oj6WgdslAa8

23

A jog to Key West

Brand had already gone "black." He had no identity, no documents. He had to smuggle himself out of the country. How could he manage it? Who might help him?

He thought of a youngster he slightly knew: Alfredo Izaguirre, hardly 20, the scion of a family prominent in journalism and politics. When the regime broke up the non-revolutionary press, Alfredo lost his position as a newspaper editor and joined the underground opposition. Brand got his American friends to set up a meeting with him.

"I have an immediate need to make a trip to the States," Brand told the other man. "I cannot leave by legal means. Can you provide me the means to do so?"

"I'm in an awkward position, Brand. I'm not sure who you really are."

"What do you mean?"

"Only this: in my efforts to verify that you are not a government agent, I have mentioned you to several people who should know you, and they do not know you."

"Mentioned me how?"

"By the name of Pancho."

In an earlier encounter, Brand had told Alfredo that he was known to some of Alfredo's friends as "Pancho." Now, with a patience rare for him, Brand started an explanation of how aliases work in the underground.

Alfredo however had no patience for it and burst out: "If I were sure you were a government agent, I would kill you where you stand – but I am not sure."

Brand took leave while wondering: *Does this fellow understand that if I were a government agent, those words would doom him?*

The matter was growing desperate. Brand sent a note to his mother-in-law Dr. S., directing her to a rendezvous with him.

Pelén's mother was not going to miss this meeting. The headstrong woman had filled up with rage at the treatment her daughter was receiving. While Dr. S. had no notion of what her son-in-law might need, her nature told her she must be the one to deal with him.

Brand was ready to talk with Dr. S. but didn't quite trust her. For all he knew, she might bring police.

When Dr. S. appeared for the rendezvous, she felt more than one gun pointing in her direction. Her perceptions were accurate; the place was indeed 'covered.'

Brand told her: "I must get out of the country by private means. I'm looking for somebody who can take me in a yacht or boat. Do you know anyone who can help me?"

The lady thought fast: "Perhaps my psychiatrist."

"Your psychiatrist!"

"He knows a lot of people with boats. Give me a day or two and call his clinic. I'll tell him to expect your call."

"How's my wife?"

"Settled in Miami."

"Everything went well at the embassy?"

"No problems. But my husband and I are also preparing to leave and we're having some problems. Maybe you can help."

"How?"

"We need dollars, and the exchange rate for pesos is very bad. Perhaps you can get us a better rate."

"How much do you need?"

"Four thousand dollars."

"Let me see what I can do."

In a few days the four thousand dollars, changed by US officials at the now-vanished rate of one for one, were in Dr. S.'s hands.

Things began to move. The psychiatrist received him warmly.

"I've set up a meeting with a colleague of mine, Dr. Prado. He can take you in his yacht. In the meantime, why don't you stay here in my clinic? It's quite safe."

Brand installed himself in a basement room and quickly found his mood being affected by strange noises around him. The noises, it became clear, were the screams of insane people whom the doctor was keeping under his care in padded cells. The peculiar, misshapen, unremitting sounds of human misery twisted Brand's insides.

"On second thought," Brand told the doctor, "I should be elsewhere."

A short while later he was standing on a street-corner in the fancy neighborhood of El Vedado. On the dot of time a mulatto in his early twenties approached him.

"You are Carlos?" the mulatto said.

"Yes," Brand said. "Who are you?"

"I come from Dr. Prado. He's waiting for us."

They drove into a modest quarter on the outskirts of the city, definitely not the doctor's neighborhood. Brand, fearing a trap, put his hand on his pistol.

At the home of the mulatto boy, Prado was waiting – a shrewd move on the doctor's part.

Prado said: "I'm leaving for Florida in a couple of days and I'll be returning a few days after that. I'll be happy to bring you back if you want."

The man was saying all the right things. Indeed, it was almost too convenient. Castro's intelligence police were expert in ploys of this kind. Prado might be a double agent.

"A return trip could work out very conveniently." Brand said. "My mission is to get Tony Varona and bring him back to Cuba. Could you provide passage for both of us?"

"Definitely."

It was a flat-out lie. Brand had no interest in the former prime minister, who had recently fled to the US. But Varona would be a big catch for Castro.

If Prado were a police agent, and if he thought Brand could lead him to Tony Varona, then Prado and his superiors would allow Brand to reach Florida. If Prado was not a double agent, the lie was harmless.

Prado: "I'm going to take you out by hiding you in the yacht."

"I don't like it," Brand said. "Before you leave, the yacht will probably be given a thorough search. I would prefer to meet you offshore. Can we arrange that?"

"A friend of mine has a beach house in Santa María del Mar. You could stay with him the night of the 4th and swim out the following morning. I can meet you a mile from the beach. Would that be all right?"

"Yes, that's much better."

Saturday, November 5, 1960. The unusually beautiful baby girl had slept soundly, giving Brand a needed night of rest. At about 5:15 a.m. Brand finished his yoga exercises and joined his hosts, a young couple, who were scanning the horizon in the direction of Havana. At about 5:45 they saw a white speck on the water, perhaps three miles away.

"I think that's it," the man said. "Let's go!"

The shore was less than two blocks away. At that hour Santa María del Mar was especially beautiful. No one else was outside. The wind was blowing and the sea choppy. Looking at those heavy waters, Brand's hosts got concerned about his making the rendezvous on time. They gave him a pair of flippers to speed his swim.

They went out to the beach and into the water, as if for a group swim in case anyone should be watching. Brand headed north. It was rough going. He had no time to pace himself. His only way to meet the boat was to do the whole swim at full speed.

When he saw the yacht passing parallel to the coast, he realized he wasn't going to make it. He pumped as hard as he could but it was no use; the boat was going to miss him by hundreds of meters. He began to swallow water and thought: "What a stupid way to die!"

Images from his life went rushing through his consciousness. Then came two especially vivid ones: his older son at six, balancing himself on a bicycle for the first time; and his youngsters, three and two, pushing dining-room chairs to sit beside him at lunch.

Brand felt a violent upsurge of strength. Looking to the open sea, he saw the yacht turn around. It was going to pass in front of him a hundred meters away.

"Prado! Prado! Prado!" he screamed.

The yacht gave a lurch and made directly for him. Prado lowered a ladder on the port side and pulled Brand onto the deck. "North! Full engine!" he cried to the skipper.

When Brand could focus again, he saw Prado's wife lounging on deck. Big with child, she was looking him over.

By the time they docked, Brand was already in the clothes he had given Prado in Havana. He borrowed some dollars from his host, took a taxi to the airport and bought a ticket to Miami under an alias. Three hours later he was kissing his two younger kids whose remembrance, along with that of their older brother, had brought him back to life.

24

Warnings

Tuesday, November 8, 1960. "You are going to fail, J.B., you are going to fail!"

The same day America was electing a new president, Brand was in Washington briefing his principal CIA contact.

"Let's not push the panic button, Brand," J.B. said back in his best aggressive-defensive manner.

The CIA was now committed to overthrowing Castro. The agency had put millions of dollars, months of effort, and its priceless reputation on the line. J.B. didn't relish the idea of going to his superiors and telling them: "One of my men has come back from the Cuban underground and says we're headed for disaster."

"Let me ask you, J.B. How many men do you have training in Guatemala?" At a group of CIA enclaves there, a Cuban force was preparing for an invasion of the island.

"In Guatemala we have close to a thousand men," J.B. said, hinting that the agency had an extra force tucked away somewhere else.

"You cannot defeat Castro with a force of that size," Brand said, ignoring the hint. "And you cannot count on the resistance to defeat Castro with help from a force of that size."

"Then what can the resistance do?" J.B. asked with an implied threat: *If your next answer does not measure up, you lose us.*

"The resistance can create chaos!" Brand said with energy. "In a moment of crisis and confusion, the people inside the government and the army who dislike Castro's policies will have their opening. They are a small minority, no question; but if they get a cue from the underground they can do something decisive. The task of the underground is to give them a clear opening – an incentive to act."

With his answer, Brand had flipped J.B. as in a judo move and pinned him to the mat. All at once the American was not speaking down to him but up.

J.B. said: "What I'm asking you to do is to go back, get your people together, locate drop-zones, let us know about them, and we'll send you what you need. The invasion force is getting restless. We can't keep those men in Guatemala much longer. We have to go faster. The heat is on. You do your part of the deal and we'll do ours."

"J.B., I'm burned," Brand replied. "In Havana I have no chance to survive more than 45 or 50 days. I think I should go to a rural area. I can move in and out of Havana, I have friends in Havana and I can act through them. But I should have my center of activity elsewhere. If not, I'm going to get caught.

"One thing more: you constantly insist that time is short. Don't send me into Cuba without weapons. I have already used lots of time looking for drop-zones and organizing reception committees. Send the weapons ahead of me. That way I can give full time to the preparation and execution of my plans."

J.B.: "This time you'll go in with your own radio operators. We have men in Guatemala preparing for your mission. You'll meet with them, be with them and see which men suit you. Two of your choice will go in with you. Pick a night with a waning moon and go in as soon as you can. We'll give you the maps. Just send us the coordinates, the exact times and the signals. We'll drop the equipment for you."

Brand: "J.B., it will not work. Don't make me waste my efforts and time. Put the weapons there first."

J.B.: "I understand what you are saying, I see your reasons, but in this matter of sending weapons ahead of you, we don't agree."

In the following days, and contrary to his fears, Brand got encouraging news. "The Viking," a man with whom he had worked closely the previous summer, now told Brand that J.B. was deeply disturbed by his report, and was giving clear accounts of it to the heads of the agency.

From other sources Brand heard sketchier stories; one of those being, "We have 25,000 men in reserve." That number could only mean the US was going to use its own troops.

A suggestive piece of evidence fell from the lips of J.B. himself: the invasion plan included a force of 30 PT boats.

That figure was important for what else it meant. The invasion force would include many different kinds of vessels. Brand, having a good grasp of military configurations, could quickly extrapolate the size of the other components. J.B. had just told him the invasion force would be huge – something in excess of a hundred thousand men, with full air support.

J.B.'s news made the difference. Brand would be in the fight whether his presence made a difference or not; whether his own group would win or not; whether he would survive or not. He was a warrior, and he felt this war pulling him in by the legs.

He had some family affairs to settle. In recent months the locus of his personal affairs had moved to the city of Miami, which had swollen with the outflow of Cubans from the island; it was already becoming another Havana. In addition to his two youngest kids and their mother, Brand had also gotten his parents to Miami, where they could live among people they had known all their lives.

Thanks to Brand's contacts, *el viejo* now had a job more in keeping with his background. He was working for the US government as an analyst, scanning newspapers and journals for trends in Spanish America. It was a big step up from carrying kitchen trays. But he was a far piece from his former self.

In Miami Brand spent as much time with the kids as he could. How it moved him, every time he came back to the house from one of his trips, to find his not-yet-three-year-old daughter Ermi short of breath, hyperventilating with excitement at his approach; and how he loved Rubén's mispronunciations, as when he showed the boy some object, saying, *"¡Rubén, mira qué lindo es!"* Rubén, look at how pretty that is!

The boy answered, *"¡Sí, qué lídon!"*

"¡Lindo, Rubén, lindo!" Father corrected.

"¡Sí, papi, lídon!"

With Pelén however his heart was finished. Like the fair-minded man he was, he held himself accountable for the distance that had grown between them and took on the task of making an honorable end.

He flew to Key West for a meeting with Pelén's father and mother, who by now had settled there. Sitting with them in a car, he said: "I've come to tell you I plan to ask for a divorce from your daughter."

Dr. S., who spoke for the family in such matters, gave back to her son-in-law a pair of lines that the authors of *Carmen* had somehow left out of their show:

"Fíjate lo que te voy a decir.
Cuídate, porque te voy a destruir."

Listen closely to what I say.
Watch out! I will destroy you some day.

25

How hard can it be?

Early in 1961 the Communist Party decided to withdraw Adolfo from Budapest and summoned him back to the political vortex. The young man was overjoyed for personal reasons as well as for the sake of his career. As he wrote to his parents, with feelings much different from those in his political discourses:

"The thing is that for some time now I've been going with a Soviet girl, and the more time I spend with her the more I'm convinced I won't find another one like her. Her name is Galina. We speak English to each other. Now she's going to study Spanish. She's already teaching me Russian. She's very intelligent, brilliant in fact; her passion is nuclear physics, which was her specialty at Moscow University. She's highly cultured. You can talk to her about anything: literature, music, cinema, painting, politics, really anything. Of course she excels over me in most of those areas, to say nothing of nuclear physics! She's 21, very short – shorter than Mom, I think – very sweet, pretty voice. In politics she's about the same as I am, although she's not a leader. I think that's the only thing I've got over her.

"You know I've wanted to marry for some time. You know me too well for explanations. If I haven't done it until now, it's because I haven't found someone who can be my wife, friend and comrade. Now I think I've found her. Why not get married? Because she isn't Cuban? I haven't found any Cuban girl like her. Because she'll have to get used to Cuba? Why shouldn't she do that? If she's in love with me, how hard can that be?"

He was about to find out. A Soviet girl in Budapest was not as easy to carry away as a nesting doll. Even as the lovers' hearts cried 'Yes!' the Soviet reply to their prayer was 'Nyet.' Adolfo had to leave for Cuba without his bride.

26

Revolutionary democracy

February 1961. The Havana to which Adolfo returned was a city preparing for war. At the airport it struck him forcibly: women and men dressed in olive-green trousers or the blue militia shirt, almost all carrying weapons. Those without pistols had submachine guns on their chests. The weapons were from Czechoslovakia; people called them *checas*, and they were everywhere.

Nearly everyone said an invasion was coming, and the regime encouraged that kind of talk; but Adolfo and his comrades kept debating it.

"The Americans will never risk a direct intervention. US imperialism would never be so foolish as to expose itself like that," said his bosom buddy César Gómez, who had come with his wife Thais to meet Adolfo's flight.

Leave it to César, to say the stuff that others wouldn't think or dare to say.

Adolfo and his two friends were going straight to the "Rebel Youth," located in the old Communist headquarters on Carlos III Avenue. It was the same building that Emi was planning to attack.[37]

In line with the regime's call to promote revolutionary unity, all political parties were letting go their identities. So the old Socialist Youth had become the Rebel Youth, a new, expanded organization

---

[37] See Chapter 19, "Red Menace," above.

that included people from Castro's non-communist July 26th Movement and the Directorio as well as Adolfo's communist comrades.

Adolfo's new assignment was to be managing director of the national youth magazine, *Mella*.[38] He already knew the Rebel Youth director, *comandante* Joel Iglesias. At just 19 a hero of the liberation war, with facial disfigurements to show for his gallantry, Joel was a short, sturdy peasant with a direct homespun style. He had no formal education – a trait Adolfo overlooked because he found the lad so decent and likeable.

"Hey, Rivero!" Joel greeted Adolfo. "Let me introduce Fernando Ravelo. You'll be working with him at *Mella*."

The two new comrades joined in the customary *abrazo*. Ravelo was a Rebel Army captain who had also been a journalist for the July 26th Movement in the Sierra Maestra – a short, neat youngster with a sparse beard and an easy smile. Ravelo had been appointed director of *Mella*. How he would share authority with Adolfo, the managing director, was an open question.

"Rivero, shouldn't we take care of your lodging?" César, a practical sort, put in. Adolfo himself had given no thought to it.

"I think we have a free room at *Mella*," Ravelo said.

Mella was located in another building nearby. The manager there showed Adolfo to an empty room that comrades on guard duty sometimes used. A toilet and shower were down the hall. The room was empty but for an old bunk bed with squeaky springs. On that bed Adolfo placed a single suitcase that contained all his earthly belongings, and he was home.

The *Mella* directors got to work with high spirits and

---

[38] Named for Julio Antonio Mella, the iconic student leader who helped establish the FEU and the Cuban Communist Party in the 1920's

camaraderie. Adolfo exerted his authority over the magazine while Ravelo, the nominal director, gave plenty of room to communist viewpoints.

§§§

A thorny issue did arise over the friendly relationship that had sprung up between Rebel Youth leaders and *comandante* Rolando Cubela. A leader of the old Directorio, Cubela had been one of the most vaunted fighters in the liberation war. Shortly after taking power Fidel had backed Cubela for president of the Havana student union (FEU). It was a surprising choice, given Fidel's hatred of the Directorio; but Cubela, a decisive actor, quickly turned Havana University into another arm of the new regime.

Cubela was very much his own man – a trait that drew antagonism from others. Adolfo and César, for their part, looked on Cubela as a kindred spirit. They also reasoned that if Cubela were prominent in the Rebel Youth, their group would benefit at the university.

César was already working at the university as a Party organizer.[39] At a directors' meeting he and Adolfo nominated Cubela to a post in the leadership of the Rebel Youth, an organization that other communists openly viewed as a private preserve.

In their motion for Cubela, César and Adolfo were vehemently opposed by Joel Domenech, who worked as assistant to Communist Party leader Aníbal Escalante. Domenech was an ambitious cadre. He seemed to speak for many communists – perhaps including Aníbal – who found Joel Iglesias conveniently easygoing and pliable. Iglesias backed up by Cubela would be another matter entirely.

---

[39] See Chapter 58, "Laurel & Hardy," below.

Adolfo and César got into an argument with Domenech. Cubela's nomination had to be put to a vote, which was rare. The motion was defeated. Adolfo and César let the matter go; they understood revolutionary democracy to mean that if you lose a vote, you lose clean.

But Domenech kept coming at them. He gestured to Adolfo and the two of them went out to a balcony facing Carlos III Avenue.

"What kind of proposal was that?" Domenech whispered with fury. "Don't you know I am the one who represents the Party here?"

Adolfo was dumbstruck. At once he saw that a hidden, conspiratorial policy was in effect – hidden even from loyal, high-ranking militants like himself. Despite the regime's move to non-partisanship, an organized Communist core was still giving directions and working to manipulate events. Domenech, crudely, had revealed it all in a phrase.

Adolfo's scalp tingled as an old warning from his brother passed through his mind: *Never depend on the Party. Never give up your freedom.*

When the Party and freedom appeared as one, that warning had made no sense. What about now? What if this incident revealed a gulf between the Party and Adolfo himself?

27

Fatherly advice

With all his preoccupations, Adolfo did not stop pining for
Galina. He kept replaying their happy times in Budapest
and wanted her by his side. He submitted a note to the Party
leadership, asking permission to have her brought to Cuba. No
less than Aníbal Escalante sent for him.

As he came into Aníbal's office, Adolfo found the large figure of a
man bristling with power and radiating friendliness. Aníbal was a
founding father of Cuban communism; his service dated back to
the salad days of the 'People's Socialist Party.' Nowadays he was
helping Fidel place Communist Party members into offices all
over the regime.

"What's going on?" Aníbal asked in a concerned way.

"Well, I, uh, fell in love with a Russian girl in Budapest and I
want to marry her. She studies atomic physics and works in a
center for nuclear research."

"Why is she in Hungary?"

"She married a Hungarian who was studying in the Soviet Union.
He brought her to Budapest. They divorced but she stayed."

Aníbal reflected for a moment, studying the young man.

"We would have no problem in sending for her," he said. "I don't
believe anyone will raise objections. Nevertheless, as you must
realize, you are not the first man who has gone to work abroad
and fallen in love."

"Yes, I'm sure that must be true," Adolfo said timidly.

"Experience tells us that, in general, those marriages do not work," Anibal said with a winning frankness. "It is not impossible that they do, but it is very difficult. Many things militate against it. The backgrounds of two people having nothing in common – their habits, their customs . . ."

Aníbal talked in this vein for some time. He paused and asked: "Did you leave her pregnant?"

"Of course not," Adolfo said.

"At least that is to the good."

Adolfo, who initially had felt strange in this dialogue, soon warmed to it. After all, communism was his life. Why shouldn't he have the advice of a Party leader? And Adolfo was quite bowled over that Aníbal, with all his responsibilities, would give him the attention. Aníbal was talking as a father might – indeed, as his own father had not.

"The choice is in your hands," Aníbal concluded.

"I think your view is completely correct," Adolfo forthrightly acknowledged.

"You will save yourself many headaches," the older man said reassuringly.

Adolfo felt immensely grateful.

28

The jump

Washington DC, early 1961. With his return to Cuba decided,
Brand still had to settle with J.B. about a weapons drop.
They reached a compromise: Brand would parachute into the
Escambray and weapons would be dropped with him. A later
drop would go to the force in Pinar del Río.

To Brand it seemed the best deal he could get, and it satisfied
him.

His next move was to Guatemala, where Cuban troops under
CIA guidance were prepping for the invasion. From the base at
Retalhuleo a plane would carry Brand, two cohorts and their stash
of weapons to a drop-point in the Escambray.

Brand chose his men and worked out final details. His American
case officer told him: "You will be the last man to go out of the
plane."

"No!" Brand replied. "Those men must see that I am the one
leading them into action, so I will jump first."

"All right," the case officer said, "but they will go out of the plane
in any case."

Brand swallowed his disgust at the comment.

Not long before takeoff the case officer told him: "If you are
caught and forced to talk, we must agree on a code."

"Hey! If I am captured I am not going to talk," Brand corrected,
and the case officer had to eat that one.

{Emi's recollections}

Two a.m., March 3, 1961. I jumped into the night and immediately felt the jerk of the parachute opening. I looked for the plane and saw it clearly as it raced across the heavens. "They didn't jump," I thought. Just then two men dropped from the plane and right after them the container of weapons and ammunition. I looked down to find the ground rushing up at me.

The hip-deep *paraná* grass in which I landed cushioned the shock like a mattress. When the breeze caught my canopy and began to drag me across the field, I pulled the right riser with both hands and collapsed the canopy. Within a minute I had removed my helmet, folded my parachute into a bundle and was ready to rejoin my comrades.

We shook hands heartily. No one had been hurt – although Mendoza, the tallest of us, had pulled on his risers so vigorously that he drove an elbow into his ribs and knocked the wind out of himself. Jorge, the youngest of us, had made a perfect jump. Both were excited and in high spirits.

I told them not to move from that spot while I searched for the reception team. With my .45 in hand I pushed through the grass in what I hoped was the direction of the fire. By design it had burned for only a pair of minutes to confirm the presence of the reception committee and coordinate the drop. With luck I saw a white spot that on my approach resolved into two men and three horses.

"Ernesto?" I called out, for that was the alias of our contact.

"No," someone answered, "but we come from Ernesto."

He handed me a match and a toothpick, the sign to be given by anyone Ernesto sent. I replaced my pistol in its holster and smacked my hands, a signal for Jorge and Mendoza to join me.

When the three of us had linked up, I asked one of our contacts whether he knew where the weapons container was.

"We saw it fall," he said, "and we think we know where to find it."

Fortunately he was right. By retracing our steps we found the container, which we then packed on one of the horses. After stashing the parachutes I instructed our contacts to hide the container in a safe place.

"Come this way," one of them said.

In about 15 minutes we had reached a sugar-cane field. Pushing through the canes, we walked a short distance to a clearing about the size of a dressing closet, barely large enough for three men to lie down. Our contacts told us to stay there for the night; in the morning they would bring food.

We lay down to sleep with our pistols by our sides. Although pistols are no match for rifles or machine guns, at times the shock of pistol-fire will cause confusion and give a chance for escape.

Jorge and Mendoza woke me several times during the night, alarmed by rustling sounds in the cane. I too had heard the noises and assumed they must be rats or other animals foraging for food. I was pleased to be awakened by my comrades, as it proved they were alert.

As promised our contacts brought food in the morning. Breakfast was welcome; we ate voraciously.

By afternoon the heat in the open field was intense. We sought relief in a nearby brook, bathing and swimming. The rest of the day and night we waited for Ernesto, all the while discussing activities we would undertake in Havana. On the second morning our contacts brought more food and the news that Ernesto, a leader of the resistance, would arrive late in the day.

At dusk they returned with Ernesto. He had prepared everything for our move. We walked for 15 minutes to a jeep and drove for about an hour to a country house, where we bathed and enjoyed a hearty peasant dinner. Over the meal Ernesto told us the weapons container was hidden in a safe place and the parachutes buried.

Very early in the morning we set off separately for Havana. It was time to put the pieces together again.

29

State of terror

Brand's chief partner in Havana was Efrén Rodríguez, the fellow attorney who had barged into his office two years earlier with exclamations about communists in the regime. Those comments had alarmed even Brand, who pressed extroversion to its limits.

Efrén, a master at demolitions, had been the author of numerous explosions in the capital that the regime could not conceal from an anxious public. Fidel's agents had him at the top of their most-wanted list and were hard on his trail.

Brand had hardly caught up with Efrén when the other man said he had to leave.

"Where to?"

"A meeting of the section chiefs."

"I don't like that!" Brand exclaimed.

"Don't worry," Efrén said, flashing his good-natured smile and clasping a charm on his neck. "The Virgin will protect me."

Next day Brand got word that Efrén's driver had seen him leave the meeting in the custody of a plainclothesman who made it look as innocuous as possible. That was State Security, keeping a low profile. Efrén had managed to signal the driver by pinching his own throat in an unmistakable gesture: I'm taken, and I'm dead.

Within several days Efrén had been shot.

Brand's Havana operation had lost its right arm. The others in Efrén's network must now regroup. It was urgent for Brand to get weapons into the city. The people in Havana could set bombs and create disruptions, but without guns they could not make a decisive move.

Brand was also getting messages from Pinar del Río: When are the guns being dropped? Brand kept asking his CIA contacts in Havana and got no answer. As a temporary measure, he could supply the men in Pinar del Río with some of the guns from Ernesto's farm.

Following Plinio's death, Brand had no major contact in the Escambray; so the Americans gave him Ernesto, a businessman with strong credentials and a likable personality. Ernesto was not a patch on Plinio, but Brand always remembered a piece of advice he'd culled from Aristotle. In politics you do not create people; you work with the people you have.

After arranging for transport of the guns from the center of the island, Brand summoned Ernesto to a meeting and told him: "I'm ready to take the weapons from your farm."

"We have a problem," Ernesto replied. "The weapons are no good anymore."

"No good! What do you mean?"

"A heavy rain swamped the ground where they were buried. The guns rusted, and they are now unusable."

"All of them?"

"All."

That could not be true. Before his drop, Brand had questioned the CIA people about how they were going to pack the guns. They had assured him the guns would be in top shape even if they had to sit for weeks in a swamp.

What was going on? It seemed Ernesto had panicked. Brand had seen it dozens of times. Well-to-do men like Ernesto just assumed they could be as effective in clandestine life as they had been in business. Then they came face to face with the pressures – horrible tensions of a kind they had never known, piling up with a speed they could not imagine.

With the state of terror that gripped the country, Ernesto had to be afraid of getting caught in a police trap. He didn't want to risk having the guns moved off his farm.

Brand thought: *What the hell, I'll give the man a few days to get over his worries. When he's cooled down he'll let me have the guns.*

30

Full orchestra

"Get up!" Brand's friend Ana shook him in alarm. "Something is going on!"

"Tell me!" Brand was alert.

"The *Ciudad Libertad*[40] is being strafed and bombed."

"How do you know?"

"Someone called and said so. What can it mean?"

Six a.m. Saturday, April 15, 1961. Massive explosions rocked the center of Havana. It must be the CIA; no other explanation was possible. But Brand had gotten no word of an attack. Neither had anyone else in the underground, as far as he knew.

Without a doubt the goal of the attack was to destroy Castro's air force in advance of a landing by troops. But why attack without sending word to the underground?

Brand knew that the Cuban force being trained in CIA camps was not nearly big enough to be preceded into battle with this massive overture. But for an American-sized intervention, the full-orchestra treatment would be just right.

Whatever their plan, the CIA was putting the underground into serious jeopardy. The bombardment would create massive

---

[40] Havana's local airport, serving domestic traffic as well as Cuba's military

confusion in the ranks. It was already sending Fidel a message he would not miss. "Make your arrests. We are coming."

31

Day of glory

April 15, early. In his room at *Mella* Adolfo was dead asleep on his bunk bed, which had grown so distressed from sagging that it was now an iron hammock on a steel frame.

He dreamt of rain pouring down on him. He thought he heard a door slam.

"Félix! Get up! They are bombing Havana!" The excited voice of his friend 'Ezequiel,' a buddy from the anti-Batista war, was calling Adolfo by his underground name.

"This is it, Ezequiel!" Adolfo cried back, using the other man's underground name. They were thrilled to be back in the fight, and not a little scared.

Adolfo clambered out of the iron hammock and pulled on his boots. From afar he could hear explosions with a musical beat. His mind was humming. He imagined himself and his friend running across a moonscape of smoky craters, past buildings on fire and huge brick walls tumbling down.

Now more than ever Adolfo felt proud to be a communist. Once again life had proved the communists correct. Who but they had understood the nature of U.S.-Cuban relations? Who but they would have known that an American attack on Cuba was inevitable?

At last the young communists had the fight they wanted. No longer would they be grey, shadowy figures of the underground; no longer would the *guerrilla* heroes of the Sierra Maestra or the gallant martyrs of the Presidential Palace look down on them.

Adolfo and his friends were no strangers to terror. For years they had lived under hanging swords. They had had to suffer danger with never a chance for glory. Now their day of glory had come.

Adolfo squeezed a Soviet-made pistol into his belt. He and Ezequiel ran down the stairs, jumped into a car and sped off toward Carlos III Avenue.

The explosions had stopped. Everything looked normal. Finding no one at the Rebel Youth offices, they went to the headquarters of the ORI, Cuba's new ruling body.[41] There they ran into Joaquín Ordoqui, one of the communist elders and a member of the ORI central committee. He was dressed in the usual olive-green uniform.

"The airports of San Antonio and Santiago de Cuba have been bombed. So has the Rebel Army headquarters," he told the young men tersely. That last had been the attack on *Ciudad Libertad.*

"So the explosions we have been hearing . . ."

". . . were not bombs but ammo dumps exploding."

"What now?" the young men asked.

"We must be alert," the old-timer answered.

"No invasion! Perhaps this isn't a war after all," Adolfo said glumly.

"Maybe it *is* a war," Ezequiel said. "The Americans must be preparing something big."

"The *revolution* is big!" Ordoqui snapped at Ezequiel, fixing him with one eye while tracking Adolfo with the other. "Imperialism is a pile of shit!"

---

[41] *Organizaciones revolucionarias integradas,* Integrated Revolutionary Organizations

The old man strode off in a foul mood, swaying side to side like a gorilla.[42]

"They will be here in 48 hours," Ezequiel muttered as if talking to himself.

"Where do you think they will land?" Adolfo asked.

"How the hell should I know?" Ezequiel gave back. "I haven't been able to speak with Kennedy yet!"

They split up and Adolfo went back to the Rebel Youth offices. Joel Iglesias, whose youthfulness always impressed Adolfo, sat at his desk rummaging through a cigar box; a huge portrait of Fidel in a beret hung on the wall behind him. Other youth leaders took their places at the meeting table as Joel sat at the head place and lit a *Cinco Vegas* cigar.

"Look, Rivero," Joel asked intently, "you studied there, you should know them. Do you think they will come?"

"I'm not sure about Kennedy. He doesn't seem like a man who would order an invasion," Adolfo said.

---

[42] Comrade Ordoqui, whom no one seemed to like very well, had trouble in his future. In March 1964 he would fall victim to Castro's purge of the old Communist Party. https://www.nytimes.com/1964/03/24/archives/cuba-seizes-a-top-communist.html It appears that Ordoqui's wife, Edith García, had acted as a Castro snitch and implicated her own husband. https://timesmachine.nytimes.com/timesmachine/1964/03/24/97174108.pdf?pdf_redirect=true&ip=0 The larger story here – which The Times' reports from Cuba during this period adroitly suggested – was Castro's steady accumulation of power at the expense of Cuba's older communists. For Fidel's two-step purge of the Party, see Chapters 44 and 53, below.

"Kennedy doesn't decide!" Domenech broke in. "Kennedy does what the military-industrial complex tells him to do! Isn't that so?" He turned his keen blue eyes on Adolfo, a good-kid smile plastered across his face.

"No!" César exclaimed. "The military-industrial complex is not a person and its opinions cannot be formed so easily!"

César actually thought the Americans made up their minds *en bloc*,[43] but he wouldn't miss a chance to tweak the upwardly-mobile communist.

Domenech took the bait. "You are the university people," he said sardonically, "the Marxist culture …"

"The university people have never been a faction," Adolfo shot back in César's defense. But he was annoyed at his friend's habit of picking a fight with Domenech.

Joel scratched his beard and mused. "What I do know is that they have lost Cuba. If they invade they lose it, and if they don't invade they also lose it."

It was not a bad reflection for a simple peasant guy.

---

[43] See the opening paragraphs of Chapter 26, "Revolutionary democracy," above.

32

A cardinal rule

April 15-16. While Adolfo and his friends were dancing on air, Brand and his friends tried to keep their hearts from crashing to the floor. Havana had become a shooting gallery and they, the government's enemies, were everyone's targets.

Military trucks, patrol and civilian cars crammed with gun-toting men raced along streets and avenues, blaring horns and sirens. Militias were being assembled or were marching through the city. Radio and TV announcements kept spreading the alarms, repeating news of bombardments across the island and warning that further attacks were imminent.

During the whole day Brand had been trying to contact friends and fellow conspirators, to see if they were still able to act and find out what means they had. He found precious little.

After dusk, hardly a person or car could be seen on the streets. The city looked uninhabited. Despite the evident risk, Brand felt he must locate Ernesto and Jorge, his radio operator. The weapons drop for Pinar del Río still had not taken place, and Brand was desperate to talk to headquarters.

Going out to look for Ernesto, Brand had decided to take with him the attractive blonde at whose apartment, a safe house, he was going to spend the night. The blonde was strongly committed to the fight and ready to do her part. She understood Brand's reasoning: her presence would keep other men distracted.

Brand managed to get in touch with a taxi service, ordered a car, and set out with his escort for Ernesto's residence a 15-minute ride away. Public buses which normally crowded the city's avenues were absent. Major intersections were empty save for patrol cars parked in a vigilant attitude, headlights turned off.

The taxi approached a fashionable neighborhood and pulled up in front of a mansion. When Brand rang, it was not a servant but Ernesto himself who answered.

"*¡Eres un salvaje!* What a beast you are, to take such a chance!" Ernesto said to Brand in astonishment.

The three of them went into the house.

"Listen Ernesto, I need to contact Jorge immediately."

"We have to wait until tomorrow."

"Not tomorrow. Jorge must have messages for me, and I also have messages to send."

Brand kept his cool but he was beyond being tired of Ernesto's negatives.

"I don't know where he is," Ernesto said. "I have to wait for him to contact me."

"But how can that be? You are the one who placed him in an apartment!"

"It's rather awkward to explain," Ernesto said, visibly disconcerted by the presence of the blonde.

"We are all friends here," Brand said. "Please speak freely. I insist."

"Okay. It happens that Jorge has been staying in an apartment belonging to a young divorced woman."

"So?"

"The young divorced woman lives with her mother."

"Can we get to it, please?"

"All right," Ernesto said petulantly. "Today the old lady threw Jorge out of the apartment."

"Why?"

"She caught him in bed with her daughter."

"I see."

In the underground it was a cardinal rule that you did not go to bed with the mistress of your safe house. Brand stole a look at his escort. She was listening without expression but he could hear the laughter pealing inside her.

"Tomorrow Jorge will tell me where he has gone," Ernesto said. "I will put you right in touch with him. I promise."

"I believe you," Brand replied. Indeed, no one could have made up such a tale.

"Now I'll call for a cab," Brand said.

"No," the other man insisted. "Let me take you wherever you're going. I don't want you to risk another cab ride."

Brand gave him directions to a corner some blocks away from the blonde's apartment. Ernesto left them there and withdrew into the desolate city. That night Brand went to bed thinking about the versatile nature of women's influence on history.

Next day, when Brand called Ernesto, the other man's first words were: "Listen, that was a very extraordinary woman you had with you last night."

33

Coronation

Sunday, April 16, 1961. The day following the air attacks was given to a solemn ceremony for the seven Cubans who had lost their lives in the bombings. Fidel had called for everyone in the country to attend.

Heeding that call, people poured into Havana from all over the island. Adolfo, deciding to watch on TV, went to Joel Iglesias's office where numerous comrades had gathered.

As soon as Fidel began speaking, the comrades tossed off comments while Adolfo paced the room. Fidel's oratorical devices were familiar to all of them; their words raced ahead of his. Regarding the Americans, he exclaimed: "What they do not forgive us is that we have made . . ."

". . . a revolution for the humble," Adolfo said under his breath.

Fidel had another idea. He raised his voice to thunder pitch, repeated the opening phrase and completed it: "What they do not forgive us is that we have made a socialist revolution under their noses!"

Adolfo turned to the screen, incredulous. At the huge rally, pandemonium had broken loose as thousands of arms, brandishing rifles, bolted upward.

The youth leaders jumped to their feet and embraced each other wildly. At last! Cuba had broken the bonds of *yanqui* domination. In that room, whether one was a socialist or a nationalist or simply a rebel with a cause, every heart and soul now beat as one.

Fidel closed his address with an order to mobilize. It was another piece of rhetoric. The masses of Cubans were already mobilized, waiting to join the fight.

After two years, through seizures of farms and industries, the nation's economy was in the government's hands; while political power, with hardly a meaningful objection, had been vested in a leadership body that a single man had designed.

Fidel had done the impossible. He had turned Cuba into a communist country. And here was the outcome – a coronation as glorious and momentous in its way as Napoleon's.

To top it off, the moment had been crafted for such a declaration. Any fears or doubts about socialism were as nothing compared to the threat of invasion; and anyone in Cuba who took exception to socialism would be a coward or traitor bringing harm to the country in a time of war.

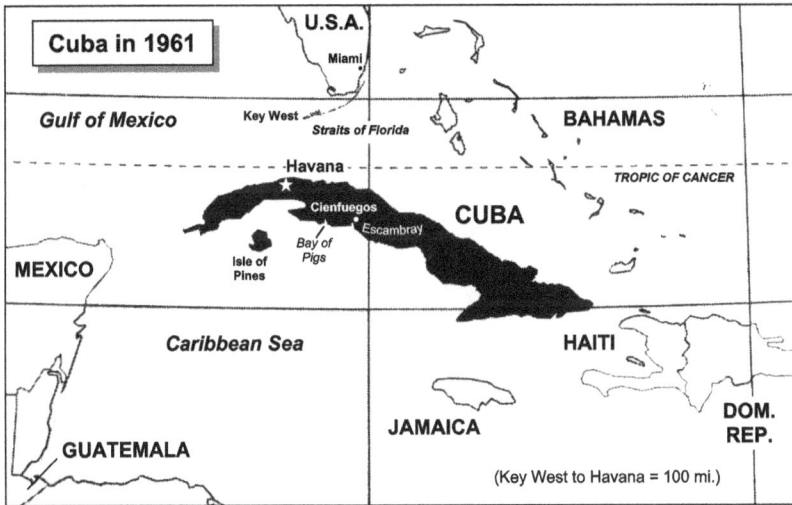

Cuba in 1961

U.S.A.

Miami

Gulf of Mexico

Key West

Straits of Florida

BAHAMAS

Havana

TROPIC OF CANCER

Cienfuegos

Escambray

CUBA

MEXICO

Isle of Pines

Bay of Pigs

Caribbean Sea

HAITI

JAMAICA

GUATEMALA

DOM. REP.

(Key West to Havana = 100 mi.)

34

Indispensable

Monday, April 17, 1961. Invasion! The enemy had landed a force at the Bay of Pigs on Playa Girón and Playa Larga, south central shore of the island.

Adolfo demanded a safe-conduct to the front as *Mella's* combat correspondent. By afternoon he had left for Santa Clara with his chauffeur Bebo, the two of them armed with *checas*[44] and ready for action.

Tuesday, April 18. The town of Santa Clara, 100 miles from the invasion, was a bedlam of uniforms and trucks. Members of the Rebel Youth were taking part in the *recogida* or mass arrest.

---

[44] See the top of Chapter 26, "Revolutionary democracy," above.

The general order was simple: imprison anyone suspected of counterrevolutionary sympathies.

People enthusiastically enforced the measure. Suspects were taken house by house, street by street, neighborhood by neighborhood. Tens of thousands of people in the city had already been jailed with no pretense of procedure. As the city's prisons couldn't hold them, they were being kept in improvised concentration camps.

The man running the *recogida* in Las Villas province was Arnaldo Milián,[45] a veteran Communist/PSP leader who specialized in agriculture. Speaking to Adolfo, he explained that the next enemy attack might be a simultaneous assault in several areas; therefore it was necessary to have reserves ready for action and to be vigilant against sabotage or efforts to block reinforcements.

Arnaldo's presentation was calm, precise, detailed and professional. Adolfo felt reassured to see the old Party coming to the fore in a moment of crisis. "The cold blood and discipline of the communists is vital to the survival of the revolution," he wrote.

San Blás. In swampy terrain close to the action, a small militia contingent was forming ranks when Adolfo and Bebo arrived. A thin young man approached with a smile. Adolfo recognized "Pijirigua," a peasant lad he had met and befriended years before at meetings of the Socialist Youth.

Adolfo's eye fell next on Major Félix Duque, a short man in a green beret who was white with road dust. The major was talking with militia officers. As Adolfo approached, Duque turned to him without ceremony and boasted: "These militia people are superb! I have never fought with better troops."

"A large number of guns are coming up toward the swamps," Adolfo said.

---

[45] https://www.ecured.cu/Arnaldo_Milián_Castro

"I'm waiting for them," Duque answered. "When they get here, we are going to turn them into dust."

Several militia soldiers nearby were trying to work a mortar. Duque went over and dropped in the first round. A sharp, dry detonation rang out, and they were in the war.

Pijirigua went to the head of the column with Duque while Adolfo fell in with the body of troops. They advanced in two columns, one on either side of the road so they could take cover quickly. The enemy was dead ahead.

A few minutes along the road they came upon a corpse in the camouflage uniform of the invaders – the body so covered with white dust that its features were barely visible. The militiamen passed by without a stop, their boots making a dull tramp on the interminable road.

"We must retreat!" a militia officer exclaimed. "This area is controlled by mercenaries." Castro's soldiers used that word on faith – believing that no Cuban would take up arms against the revolution unless paid by Americans.

As Adolfo was thinking how sensible retreat might be, Pijirigua ran up and said excitedly: "We're advancing!"

Wednesday, April 19. "The enemy troops are now against the beach. They have broken ranks. Let's go!" Pijirigua called out.

Adolfo and Bebo went with Pijirigua to witness the end of the battle. Near San Blás they found a company of militia spread out over a field, scavenging. Among the bushes, enemy soldiers had strewn empty cans and dark tablets that looked like soap.

"Those are K-rations," Pijirigua said proudly. "I learned that during training."

A little farther along they found a Browning pistol which Adolfo's friend was happy to claim. Rebel Army troops were tearing a silk parachute into strips for souvenirs. Adolfo would have loved to have one, but he refrained because he was not a combatant.

Near Playa Girón two men in camouflage uniforms came walking out of the field with their hands raised. Adolfo stared at them in cold hatred. Those men were the Enemy. They had come to shed the blood of his comrades and restore Cuba as a *yanqui* colony.

Even though the soldiers had surrendered themselves, Adolfo thought about shooting them.

One of the prisoners, a sturdy fellow with a short haircut, said: "They left us in the lurch. This has been hell."

The comment about the Americans rolled off the prisoner's tongue in Cuban vernacular. Adolfo was ready to blow his top. A CIA mercenary had no right to sound like a Cuban.

The prisoner and his companion, a very tall thin man, were dehydrated, their lips severely cracked. Pijirigua tossed his water bottle to them. They drank desperately.

"Thanks," the taller one said. "It's a strong sun here. I'm from La Víbora. Where're you from?"

La Víbora was a lower-middle-class neighborhood in Havana. Adolfo was not about to say he was from El Vedado, a neighborhood quite a bit fancier than that of his captive.

"Get into the jeep," Adolfo answered with scorn, pointing with his *checa*. "You are my prisoners, not my guests."

Saturday, April 22. A group of youth directors including Adolfo went to meet with President Dorticós and other leaders at the Presidential Palace. As usual Fidel was there, thinking aloud in a stentorian voice. He spent many words praising the air force for sinking the enemy's supplies at sea. From out of nowhere he brought up Major Félix Duque, whom Adolfo had mentioned in his account for *Mella*.

"He is always thinking about how to make himself conspicuous, how to call attention to himself," Fidel said. "Duque is one of those men who do not accept the lowly place in history to which their own mediocrity condemns them."

Adolfo found the statement terribly rough. On the beaches Duque had been a gallant, heroic defender of the revolution. If Fidel so resented that man whom he knew as a faithful subordinate, how must he feel about the simple soldiers, workers and peasants under his command?

But no, Fidel had a point. Duque was a soldier, a fine soldier, maybe even an exceptional soldier – but in the end he was dispensable as every soldier must be. Fidel was Fidel, indispensable. Adolfo and his comrades were so many men among many others. Fidel was unique, everyone in one.

35

A passable evening

{from Emi's recollections}

Sunday, April 23, 1961. I decided to spend the afternoon at the
El Vedado apartment of Adela, a widow in her late thirties who
lived with her white-haired mother. When I dropped by, they
were having a late lunch and invited me to join them.

Like most Cubans they had been following the dramatic events of
those days on radio and television. They did not know the extent
of my involvement in clandestine activities, but they understood
I had a lot on my mind; so after a long and pleasant conversation
they suggested I use their back bedroom to read and nap.

I accepted their kind offer and retired to the bedroom. Out of
concern that my hostesses might be alarmed at the sight of a gun,
I put my pistol on a shelf behind a row of books.

Immersed in reading, I noticed raised voices from the living
room. It sounded like an argument. I walked down the hall to the
living room and asked, "What's wrong, Adela?"

In a dismayed voice Adela said, "It's the police." At that instant I
became aware of a man pointing a submachine gun at me.

Actually it was not the police but State Security; three agents
commanded by a lieutenant in his early twenties. With them was
a fifth man, a prisoner who had guided them to the apartment – a
snitch.

In putting my pistol aside as a concession to the feelings of my
hostesses, I had ignored another cardinal rule. Had I ruined my

chances for escape? Or unwittingly saved my own life by ruling out a firefight?

My captors heard from me a carefully prepared story which had some grains of truth. I was a freelance journalist for CBS television news and for *The New York Times*. I expected to sell my reports on Cuba for substantial sums.

"And did you need this for your reporting?" the lieutenant asked, pointing to my pistol which they had found in a quick search of the house.

I replied: "We have all seen the climate of unrest, confusion and violence in the country. I have simply carried that pistol for my own protection."

The lieutenant obviously didn't believe my story, but at least it had given me something to say that did not antagonize him or compromise the two women.

The Security men kept us all in the apartment for some hours. Either they hoped to entrap someone else or they preferred not to show an arrest in daylight.

One of the many things that went through my mind in those hours was the conversation in which I had told J.B. that I would have 45 days in Havana, 50 tops, before getting arrested. This was the 51st day of my return to Cuba.

My paramount concern was to help the two women who had been so kind to me. As it turned out, the mother had similar feelings toward me. When one of the agents threatened her, she said: "I am an old woman. I have lived enough. I don't care about myself. But I do care for the lot of this man who is in the bloom of his life."

Perhaps my story distracted the agents, because although they searched the house they forgot an elementary police measure: they didn't search me. That was fortunate because my shirt pocket contained three very thin strips of paper on which I had written messages to give my radio operator for relay to the United States.

When after dusk I was walked to the Security car half a block away, I managed to pull out the papers, wad them into a ball and toss them into the grass along the sidewalk.

At State Security headquarters I was ordered to sit on a bench in a hallway. While there I witnessed the frequent coming and going of numerous homosexuals who were identifiable from their voices and their exaggerated gait.

They were dressed in everyday casual clothes but obviously worked for the G-2.[46] Most of them looked excited, visibly rejoicing in their work as informers, surely because it enabled them to strike back at a society that had scorned them.

I sat on the bench for two hours with no one questioning or even approaching me. Around 11:30 p.m. someone came to fetch me and guided me to a small office, where a desk and four chairs occupied almost the entire space.

Waiting there for me was the boss of Castro's counterintelligence[47] whom everyone, for the obvious reason, called Redbeard. With him was the arresting officer, identified as Lieutenant Cuenca, plus a young captain whose name was not mentioned.

I was placed in a chair facing Redbeard. All lights were turned off except for a lamp on the desk which was directed upwards into my face from only four or five inches away. That seemed to me a ridiculous bit of Hollywood drama.

Redbeard began with general inquiries about my activities. I repeated that I was in Cuba as a freelance journalist.

---

[46] State Security officers
[47] *Comandante* Manuel Piñeiro Losada

"That looks like a front for the CIA," he said.

To establish my revolutionary sentiments, I began what turned into a monologue on revolutions in general and the Cuban revolution in particular. I asserted that the struggle against Batista had been a political one and that Castro, in superimposing a different agenda on the revolution, was creating a schism that could have been avoided.

The masses, I asserted, had been fed a legend about the revolution that did not correspond to the facts. The revolutionaries against Batista – and I identified myself as one of the first – mostly supported the laws put into effect by Castro's government. We were just not ready to accept a communist regime.

As I told my interrogators: "The communists didn't join the fight against Batista until victory was in sight." The American press, I added, found the subject very juicy; I intended to score a journalistic coup and make lots of money with my reports.

While talking I managed to inch the lamp away from me and direct it toward the wall without raising objections from my captors.

Having mentioned communism, I spoke about Russia – its history since the time of Yemelyan Ivanovich Pugachev's revolt in the 18th century, the peasant uprisings of the 19th century, the Russo-Japanese war of 1905, Trotsky's role in the 1905 revolution, the "Potemkin" incident where food protests led to an unexpected twist; then the massive events unleashed by World War I, the February 1917 toppling of the czar, Kerensky's government, Lenin's ride in an armored train across Germany, his arrival in Petersburg, his going underground; "Today is too soon, the day after tomorrow will be too late;" the "ten days that shook the world;" Lenin in power, agrarian reform, Lenin the realist advising acceptance of peace, the treaty of Brest-Litovsk, the civil war, Trotsky and the Red Army, the shooting of Lenin, his convalescence, recovery, stroke and death, the testament, Stalin's grasping for power, purges.

Throughout my monologue I felt somehow mortified by a deficiency in my critical analysis of communism. Though I had read much of Lenin's writing, I had read little of Hegel, Marx, Engels and others whose works were essential to a good understanding of the subject.

That deficiency seemed not to bother my captors, who listened attentively throughout. At least I had avoided a real interrogation and turned what could have been a very unpleasant evening into a passable one.

Redbeard concluded the interview by saying: "Doctor, we need people like you to give lectures to our men." In the circumstance I took it as a compliment.

I was sent to a room that had been converted to a cell. It held twenty men. There I slept on the floor during my first night as a prisoner.

Part Three

Trials

36

The yogi

When Security agents raised their guns against him, Brand was dead and Emi Rivero reborn – to pass a lifetime in jail, if he was lucky.

May 15, 1961. From the prison at La Cabaña fortress, where he had spent three weeks after his interrogation by Redbeard, Emi was transferred back to the caviar of penal accommodations – the 'galleries' at State Security headquarters, now much more crowded than before.

He drew Cell Three, packed to the limit with about fifty men. Three-tiered bunks had been carelessly placed around the big room. A hole in the floor with a shower-head above it was the only sanitary facility for all fifty.

While introducing himself to the others in the cell, Emi was called out and led to a room where an officer sat behind a large desk. The officer motioned Emi to sit down opposite him.

"The G-2 already knows quite a lot about you but we need to know more. How did you enter Cuba? What were your most recent activities?"

"I am a freelance journalist, trying to sell articles to CBS television and *The New York Times*. Since I wanted to make the reports without the government's knowledge, I came to the country as a stowaway on a freighter from Central America."

"Your story is not believable."

"I have spoken with Mr. Richard Eder of *The New York Times* about filing my reports. If you have any doubts about what I am saying, you can contact Mr. Eder and check for yourself. He likes to talk to Cuban officials and he speaks perfect Spanish."

The officer took up a ballpoint pen and said: "If you tell me that this pen is made of solid gold and invite me to check it to convince myself, I don't have to check it because I know the pen is not gold."

Emi Rivero, who did not scare easily, found the statement unnerving.

The officer said: "Do you know what dooms you? Let me tell you: it is your lawyer's mentality. What counts at the trial is not what the president of the tribunal might say, or the prosecutors or your lawyers or witnesses or evidence or any of that. What counts is what the G-2 says. Cooperate with us, and we might take a favorable view of your case."

"I'm in Cuba trying to do the freelance reports I just mentioned."

The officer called a guard, and Emi was taken back to confinement.

Special Interrogation Facility a.k.a. "The little cabins," near Havana, August 1961:

In his tiny one-man cell – the "little cabin," as he called it – Emi continued the practice of yoga that he had regularly kept up through clandestine life. Under the intensified pressure of captivity he lengthened his sessions. Evidently the guards and officers observed his exercises through the peephole, for at times he heard various men refer to him as "el yogi."

A day or two after Emi's arrival, a pair of soldiers came into his cabin while another stood outside holding a rifle. That was the procedure for going to the bathroom, but he had not asked for the bathroom. One of the soldiers put a towel around his head and guided him down some stairs.

When his face was uncovered he found himself in a room that contained a small liquor bar. Glass doors faced out onto the residence's terrace and backyard. After the furnace-like atmosphere in his "cabin" the air-conditioning in the room felt marvelously cool on his skin.

Two young men introduced themselves as members of the G-2. The taller one, superior in rank, took the lead.

They sat down at the bar. Asked about his clandestine arrival in Cuba, Emi repeated his story about being a freelance reporter and coming by boat.

At the end of Emi's monologue the senior officer coolly said: "Brand, you are in a very dangerous position. We know how you came to Cuba – not in a ship but in an airplane, and not as a stowaway but as a parachutist. If you want, I'll pull out a map and show you the farm where you landed."

Emi kept his face immobile but he was gripped by a blinding wrath. Someone had talked, and in some detail.

"Our information is enough to take you to the firing squad," the senior man added. "Your only chance of saving your life is to give us detailed information about all your activities – contacts, arms caches, all of it. Either you tell us what we want to know, or you go to the firing squad."

"I don't know what you are talking about," Emi replied.

The interrogators left the room in a pique. The guards who had brought him downstairs reappeared with a towel, and back upstairs he went.

A few days later the peephole opened and someone snapped: "Brand!"

Emi acted as if he had not heard. The door opened and again two uniformed men appeared with a towel.

Downstairs the officers were already seated at the bar. The senior man started. "Look, Brand . . ."

"My name is Rivero."

The officers exchanged a serious look.

"We don't want to execute you," the senior man said. "You can save your life by collaborating with us. We know your friends are hiding many armaments. I propose that we take you to a telephone. You call and tell your people they should run because the G-2 is going there. You give us the address, your friends escape, we confiscate the weapons and you save your life."

"I don't know about any weapons and I don't have information to give you," Emi answered.

Again the officers looked at each other.

"What can you tell us about your brother?" the junior man asked.

"He's a dedicated communist. He spent about a year in Hungary. We had a conversation a year ago. I told him: 'Look, I don't like your being a communist but since you are one, I want you to reach the highest positions in the Party's hierarchy. I want you to succeed.' His answer to me was, 'I don't want you to succeed.'"

The interrogators laughed. "Your brother has a clear mind," the junior officer said.

Once more the towel was placed over Emi's head and he was taken back to his room.

In light of his basic motive – give no help to the G-2 – Emi was in a trap that would be difficult to leave alive. The G-2's knowledge of "Brand" and how he had entered Cuba was more than enough to place him under sentence of death. On the other hand the G-2 officers had brought up something of possible help to him: the subject of his brother.

Emi well knew the admiration and love that the regime's topmost leaders felt for his brother. By portraying his brother sympathetically, Emi might have made those Security men less interested in executing him.

They brought him for a third interview. Emi kept evading questions, turning the conversation toward politics. He talked a lot about Triple-A, the group with which he had worked in the war against Batista; specifically, how the Triple-A's recruitment of army, navy and police officers had helped bring about Batista's fall – not so much by overthrow as by a general collapse of morale.[48]

"If you decide to cooperate with us," the junior officer said, "we can put you to work as an agent inside prison. We would pay you for your work. In time you would earn large amounts of money."

"Don't offend me!" Emi snapped back.

The next interview began with another warning.

"The department is expecting results from these sessions," the senior officer said. "It is disappointed to receive little more than your analysis of the situation in which Cuba finds itself."

"That may be," Emi said, "but the department would do well to pay attention. I believe the American government will not indefinitely accept a Cuban regime that works for the Soviet Union."

"This is useless. You know what we want. You have refused to cooperate. Does anything else come to mind? We are willing to listen."

The question caught Emi off guard. "Could you give me a little time to think it over?"

"All right," the senior officer said, and they left.

---

[48] See Chapter 4, "Keep up your guard," above.

Back in his room Emi had something to ponder.

His interrogators had tried to use his survival instincts for their purposes. Why not turn the tables and use *their* survival instincts for *his* purposes?

Everyone, officials and citizens alike, feared a second invasion was coming. That alone gave Emi plenty of room for turning the tables. Instead of talking about his own life – not a promising subject – he would do better to focus on the insecurities of his captors.

"So what have you thought about our suggestion?" the junior man said when Emi was back at the bar.

"I have a proposal for you."

The men from G-2 gave their attention.

"Mark my words: the United States is planning to invade Cuba and sweep away the revolutionary government. But it seems we still have time to prevent such a thing from happening. I believe I can be instrumental in mediating an agreement between the United States and Cuba."

The senior officer asked: "What level can you reach?"

"The White House."

The questioners made no comment.

"I am ready to act as a negotiator," Emi said. "I am certain an agreement is attainable."

"We don't have an answer for that. We have to consult the department," the senior officer said.

With that, Emi was taken from the air-conditioned room and brought back to his little cabin.

37

Danger

{from Emi's recollections}

Special Interrogation Facility. After a few days I was taken back to the barroom. As soon as I saw my interrogators I could sense their tension and hostility.

"Your proposition has not been accepted," the senior officer said. "The department has determined that you are trying to take us for a ride. We cannot allow that. We must make sure you get exactly what you deserve."

My chief interrogator had announced my death sentence.

I answered that I regretted the decision, that I thought a good opportunity was being lost, and that I had nothing more to say.

From out of nowhere the senior officer said: "For you, danger is a sport."

Adolfito had said that to me a year or two before. I remembered the comment because it had hurt me. An interrogator using that same phrase could not be a coincidence. He had spoken with my brother.

In the face of my silence, the senior officer asked: "Are you thinking of telling the revolutionary tribunal the same stories you have been telling us?"

"I don't know," I said off-handedly. "It might be that I go mute and not say a word."

They took it in without reaction and left.

I was not summoned for another session. After eight or ten days a guard opened the peephole and shouted: "Brand, get ready. You are leaving."

The door opened. I was handed my clothes and shoes. After I had dressed, a towel was put around my face; I was taken downstairs and out of the house to a parking lot. I was shown to a truck, placed in the rear compartment which had no windows or seats, and driven away.[49]

---

[49] A version of this narrative appears in Adolfo Rivero Caro & Emilio Adolfo Rivero Caro, *Las cabañitas/The Little Cabins*, Miami: Alexandria Library, 2012 (twin Spanish and English volumes).

38

Uncertainty

Havana, September 17, 1961. After three days at the Department of Internal Investigations Emi was put back in a Security cell, which after a month at the "little cabin" had a family-like feel.

Shortly afterward he was rousted from the cell and taken to a cubicle where an officer was saying over a phone: "No! The problem is that his mother came to see him!" A guard with a machine gun entered. "Take him!" the officer snapped at the guard.

The guard led Emi down a hall, scolding him all the while: "You get into problems! You create problems!" They turned a corner and he was guided into an enclosure. There, behind some bars, he saw his mother with her younger sister Gloria.

"¡*Vieja!* Why did you come?

"Don't ask me such a thing!"

Delia looked at her emaciated son. The heat and dehydration at the special interrogation facility had cost him some 40 pounds in 30 days.

"How is it with you?" she asked.

"I have been through a lot, but with my chin up."

"Good. That's the only thing I want to hear."

La vieja was really tough – as tough as he'd ever seen her.

"You and *el viejo* have to prepare yourselves. I am going to be executed."

"We are doing many things for you. Your father is flying to Mexico to see the president. And your friends are helping a great deal."

They were talking in front of the guard who stood a few feet away. Her last comment was a reference to the CIA.

"I want to send a cable to my children," Emi said, addressing his mother and also the guard.

"Write the cable and show it to me," the guard said.

A pen and paper were nearby. Emi took up the pen and wrote: "Dear Rubén, Take good care of your sister. Dear Ermi, Your voice was always my music."

He gave the paper to his mother who showed it to the guard. The guard nodded approval and told the two of them to wrap it up.

"*Vieja*, be brave. I am going to be executed."

"I am a woman. I know how to be a woman. Your father is a man. He knows how to be a man."

After the meeting *la vieja* wrote to her husband: "Emi is very thin, but I thought his face looked well. His state of mind was good and I didn't fall into one of my bad moments, which fortified him. I don't know where I got the strength. God helped me."

In letters to her husband, Delia was also able to give news of her younger son whom she had not seen since leaving for the US. "I must confess that despite the immense happiness it gave Adolfito to see me, he was very cruel with me, so hard as to be abnormal."

Indeed, when *la vieja* told Adolfo about her visit to Security and spoke of Emi's high spirits, Adolfo snapped at her: "Let us see how your son's legs tremble when they put him in front of the firing squad!"

La vieja struggled to believe that Adolfo's attitude was a passing one. As she wrote to *el viejo*: "I ask God to erase these things so I may forgive Adolfito with all my heart. Be certain I will muster all the decency I can to see him in another light."

Emi was now a problem that Adolfo wanted out of the way. Apart from the political tensions of the moment and Adolfo's concern for his own standing as a Party cadre, the younger brother was also approaching a juncture that filled him with trepidation. His beloved Galina would soon arrive from Hungary and the two were to marry. Adolfo had decided to bring her in spite of Aníbal's earlier advice and his own assent to it.

Galina's flight was scheduled to arrive on a day when Adolfo would be traveling outside the country. So he said to his mother: "Listen *vieja*, since you'll be here anyway, could you go to the airport and receive Galina in my place?"

"Of course," *la vieja* said without hesitation.

"By the way," Adolfo added, "when you speak with Galina I would prefer that you not tell her about certain family matters."

La vieja answered: "My family matters begin with me and end with your father. In any case they are none of your business."

39

The academy of hatred

{Emi Rivero's recollections}

La Cabaña fortress, Havana, 2 a.m., September 22, 1961.
Summoned by a loud crash, most of the hundred men in Galera
16 crowded up to the double-barred window which looked out
onto the execution ground 50 yards away.

The giant cell filled up with screams: "Monsters!" "Sons of
whores!" *"¡Viva Cuba libre!"* Then we heard: "Aim!" "Fire!" Many
of the executed died with the name of Christ on their lips. After a
burst of fire and the *coup de grace*, we heard the sound of a truck
leaving with a corpse and coming back for another one.

My trial had just ended. I had been in a group of 62 men and six
women who had come before Revolutionary Tribunal Number
One at La Cabaña fortress – Case Number 238 of 1961. Now in
the wee hours, four people from Case 238 had been killed in the
span of 30 minutes.

The proceedings had opened at 8 a.m. in one of the big meeting
rooms of the fortress. Some 300 people crowded into the room:
accused and their lawyers, judges and prosecutors, soldiers,
journalists, defendants' relatives, and members of the diplomatic
corps –a young British businessman, Robert Morton Geddes,
being among the accused.[50]

---

[50] https://api.parliament.uk/historic-hansard/lords/1961/nov/08/cuba-
sentence-on-mr-geddes

A revolutionary mob was also on hand to provide a "spontaneous" demonstration against the accused if it should prove helpful.

In the crowd were my mother and my aunt Gloria. As I entered, they smiled at me to show confidence; but they were appalled by the grief of so many.

The tribunal was made up of its president, plus three Rebel Army men and a member of the militia. The president, Lieutenant Pelayo Fernández, was called "Pelayo Firing Wall." The prosecutor, Fernando Flores, was nicknamed *Charco de sangre,* "Pool of Blood."

The first to give evidence were G-2 agents who testified against the accused. One of those, introduced as Agent Idelfonso Canales, was the interrogator whose comment about the ballpoint pen had made a strong impression on me.

Agent Canales testified that I had been one of the first to conspire against the government and that I didn't properly belong in this group, but in another that had come to trial some months before.

Following the agents' testimonies the accused were questioned by the tribunal one at a time. Each defendant was asked, first of all, to declare guilty or not guilty.

Some of the accused disputed the charges against them; others gave vague answers. At times the president asked: "Do you ratify the statements you have already made under interrogation by State Security?" The defendant answered: "I do." Those statements were not disclosed at the trial.

Among the accused was the man whose betrayal of the apartment in El Vedado had led to my arrest. His name was Pedro Cuéllar. After spending hours in his company on that day, I had encountered him again in one of the large cells where we had both been guests of State Security. Our hosts had evidently put the two of us there to observe our relationship and gather more evidence on us.

In Security Cuéllar had behaved unpleasantly to the other prisoners, bossing them around and saying he would soon become an official of the revolutionary government. He never mentioned that he was expecting this reward for having turned a snitch. It became clear only at the trial, when he testified against many other men to devastating effect.

About me, however, Cuéllar gave no testimony at all. By a stroke of fortune he had not remembered who I was. In the Security cell I had ignored him because to do anything else would have helped our captors, and would have put me in the very mess that Cuéllar was now making for others.

When the trial broke for lunch, visitors of the accused naturally tried to come near. Soldiers blocked their way with rude exclamations, but my mother just walked through them and got close to me.

"What do you think?" she said.

"I am going to be executed," I told her.

"No! No!" she exclaimed. "Your brother says you should not speak a word."

That was a piece of news. Maybe *la vieja* thought Adolfito was trying to help. I didn't think so. I was pretty sure I was going to die, and pretty sure he knew it. But then he got concerned that I would make a scene in front of the judge and give him a bad name.

When my turn came to testify I stood before the tribunal. The president had been one of my fellow conspirators against Batista; friendship had existed between us. When he asked the ritual question of how I wanted to declare, I said: "I abstain."

That day I was the only defendant to abstain. "You may return to your seat," the president said. Within the constraints of his office, I felt he was treating me decently.

As soon as the testimonies had ended, the prosecutor made his argument. He demanded the death sentence for six of the accused. Wives, relatives and friends of those men began to wail. The president repeatedly slammed his gavel, ordering silence. The commotion went on for several minutes.

Surprisingly the prosecutor did not ask the death penalty for me but rather a 30-year prison term. Geddes, the British defendant, got the same sentence.[51]

But for the stool-pigeon Cuéllar the prosecutor demanded death.

With all the sentences announced, the president asked if any of the accused had anything to add to their statements. Cuéllar stepped forward. He was arrogant and mean as usual but his voice now had a very wide tremolo, full of fear. He said the prosecutor should not have asked the death penalty for him since his was a special case.

The president bluntly replied that the prosecutor knew what he was doing.

Cuéllar, it seemed, was one of the few not to realize that that the proceeding had been a mock trial – a *mise-en-scène* with everything scripted in advance. Accusation, verdict and sentencing had all come from the same place.

The very thing against which we had rebelled – a sovereign state in which only one opinion counts – was the thing that now held us in its grip. If the state wanted us to go to prison, we were going to prison. If the state wanted us to die, we were going to die.

---

[51] Under pressure from the UK, Geddes was released less than a year and a half later. https://www.britishpathe.com/video/ VLVA3NAH5Z8HJENTSAL5SCZUUC7AM-MEXICO-CITY-ARRIVAL- OF-THREE-BRITONS-RELEASED-FROM-CUBAN-PRISON/query/ Geddes

From the courtroom, soldiers and militia escorted us to the yard inside the fortress. All the while, the revolutionary mob hurled insults at us.

Most disturbing of all were the crowds of small children, mimicking the cries of the adults and carrying toy submachine-guns. They were beginners in the Academy of Hatred.

We were halted in the middle of the courtyard and six names were called – those of the men condemned to die.

It was a very hard moment for all of us. The six climbed onto the bed of an army truck; they were being driven off to the cells where they would await execution. As the truck pulled away, one of the condemned men – Juan Rojas Castellanos, a former Rebel Army captain who had become my friend in prison – yelled, "Rivero."

It was a one-word goodbye. I raised my arm in response.

On its way to the execution grounds, the truck stopped near a bridge where spectators from the public had gathered to watch the shootings. In that group were two young women. One of them said she wanted to leave but her friend told her: "Stay, stupid! It's going to start any minute."

That exchange was audible to the men in the truck. One of the men cried out: "Don't go away, miss! We'll give you a good show!"

The young women lowered their heads.

One of the condemned men, Rafael García Rubio, had his sentence commuted at the last instant to 30 years. It was he who told us the story.

I got back to *Galera* 16 at about 10:30 p.m. In spite of silence having been ordered as usual at 9 p.m., many inmates were still awake. I had been the only one in the *galera* who had gone to trial that day. The others had stayed up to wait for my return.

Though knowing I was not religious, they had recited the rosary for me. When I came in, some of the men simply asked: "Would you like a hot chocolate?" It was quickly prepared.

Most of the prisoners in *Galera* 16 had been military men in Batista's army or persons of high rank in his regime – *esbirros*, as they were scornfully called. For seven years I had risked my life trying to overthrow a government that those men served and defended.

When I was transferred to *Galera* 16 I made a point of trying to befriend them. What was past was past. Now we had before us an even more terrible enemy.

The men had responded to my overtures. Even those who didn't become my friends were gracious with me. On the night of my trial many of them had prayed for my life; and I was moved by their concern.

After the executions had ended, many of us stayed awake in silence. Unavoidably perhaps, I looked back over my life and at the choices I had made: to fight against Batista's regime and then to oppose the revolution when Castro turned it into an instrument of his personal power.

Even if my efforts on behalf of the revolution had misled me, I felt my choices added up to a coherent path, an intelligent life. And I was sure about the allies I had chosen in the latest phase of the struggle. To my mind it was inconceivable that the Americans would abandon or betray us.

40

Glorious city

1961. On October 5, a few days after Emi had reached his long-term prison on the Isle of Pines, *la vieja* went to visit him, taking the long trip by bus and ferry to Cuba's second-largest island.

She carried vitamins and also a bedroll, since prison bedding was no more than a strip of canvas hung between bunk rails – a canvas that also happened to be a paradise for fleas. In the prisoners' phrase, "A jail without fleas is like a marriage without children or a people without music."

La vieja did not contain her sadness at seeing Emi in a political prisoner's khaki uniform, with a tin cup attached to his epaulette. At the end of a letter to *el viejo* describing her prison voyage, Delia permitted herself to say: "I'm exhausted in spirit and body."

Her chores in Cuba were not yet over. Galina was arriving and *la vieja* would meet her at the airport. In anticipation la vieja wrote to her husband: "I do not think of telling her about disagreeable things, and certainly not about her brother-in-law . . . She is not to blame, and perhaps she will be more human" – Adolfo's name gracefully omitted.

La vieja took an instant liking to the Russian girl and showed her around Havana, which proved a major surprise for the visitor. As a Soviet student Galina had learned that Cuba was a backward country, a parvenu in the socialist world, at the very start of its development.

The experience of Havana, a modern metropolis full of beauty and riches, knocked her for a loop. On top of that was the physical splendor – warmth and sunshine, infinite horizons, the

Caribbean's colors, all imbued with a humming musicality. This was the developing world indeed; and putting the Soviet Bloc in the rear-view mirror was just the right move.

To top it off, *la vieja* presented the girl her own engagement ring before going home to Miami. It was the warmest of welcomes; and however dimly Adolfo perceived it, a robust endorsement that neither of Emi's wives had received.

41

How much for lentils?

1961. Adolfo settled Galina into his new place, a single room with a small kitchen and a balcony a block from Fidel's office.

It was a very happy reunion. Soon they were both hard at work; he on Party matters and she as a teacher of Russian language, for which a large market in Cuba now existed. When they came together at day's end, Adolfo found himself sharing a bed with someone whose stack of nighttime reading was even taller than his.

Galina had a curiosity that reached into many areas. For one thing, she wondered why her home lacked certain elementary comforts like a telephone or a refrigerator; since Cuba looked to her like a wealthy society and her man was an important cadre.

When she mentioned these things to Adolfo, he answered indifferently. Material considerations had no part in his world of ideas.

In the eyes of Adolfo and his socialist comrades, the politics of the country were advancing decisively. The communists were at the center of an effort to reorganize the country and its economy on openly socialist lines. Aníbal was now in full partnership with the commander-in-chief.

Adolfo accompanied Rebel Youth leader Joel Iglesias to a meeting with Aníbal and Fidel. It was their old comrade Domenech who admitted the youth leaders to Fidel's office; for Aníbal's assistant had now become Fidel's assistant.

As everyone sat down, Domenech took his post by the bank of

telephones. Along the bookshelves, already bound, were Fidel's collected speeches.

{from Adolfo's recollections}

Fidel had made himself director and chief expert in every field. While Joel and I had asked to see him about matters concerning the Rebel Youth, Fidel preferred to talk about his subject of the moment, which happened to be the agricultural economy.

In Fidel's view, certain beans and grains had too high a price in global markets. When Fidel spoke of beans and grains, you couldn't imagine anything in the world quite as crucial or captivating.

Abruptly the talk stopped when Fidel – whose memory was a steel trap – somehow failed to remember a figure. Domenech took up a phone, dialed a number, whispered into the receiver and gave the phone to Fidel. "*Comandante*, it is the INRA director." [52]

Fidel took the phone and said without preambles: "Listen, what is the per-pound price of lentils in the international market?"

He got the answer and gave the receiver back to Domenech. "Yes," he told his listeners, "it is . . . pesos, and if you compare with black and red beans, you'll see . . ." – and so on without a thought to INRA's director, who at that moment must have been breathing a sigh of relief for having not failed Fidel.

"The dietary habits of the Cuban people are absolutely erroneous," Fidel kept going. "We have inherited from Spain the feeding habits of a cold climate, while here we need lots of greens, lots of fruit, lots of fish . . ."

"Stews, *fabadas*," Aníbal whispered, musing over the delights of old-fashioned Spanish cuisine.

---

[52] National Institute of Agrarian Reform

"Yes Fidel, but it is very tasty!" Joel said with a guileless laugh, speaking aloud what Aníbal had whispered.

"Rice, for instance," Fidel went on without paying attention, "has all the nutritional value in the husk and we take it off to eat the grain. It would be good for us to save the money we spend to import rice and instead buy corn flour, which is much cheaper and has more nutritional value."

The unexpected topic of books came up. Someone mentioned Lenin's complete works in 75 volumes.

"I have not written much," Fidel said, "but in regard to speeches" – pointing to the volumes along the walls – "I think I'll soon get to 75 volumes."

"Those are also creations," Aníbal said, "and here they have served a very direct political purpose."

"Yes," Fidel smiled. "Those have been the injections that you must give the people periodically in order to raise their defenses."

Domenech whispered something to Fidel. They were about to close the meeting without the Rebel Youth matters having been mentioned.

Joel leapt into the breach. "Look, Fidel! We need to talk about some problems!"

Happily those matters took only seconds to resolve.

Fidel and Aníbal were going out to lunch at a Spanish restaurant, La Zaragozana. "Those people do not know how to make *cachelos*," Fidel said about La Zaragozana's cooks as we all exited the leader's office. *Cachelos* are a scramble of pork sauce, ham, bacon, potatoes, onions and red peppers.

"Yes, they must be taught," Aníbal agreed.

No one seemed to notice the variance between Fidel's earlier talk and his interest in the classical Spanish dish – but what did it matter when the Party leader and the commander-in-chief got on so well?

42

Rehabilitation

1962. Cuba's young communists were sitting on top of the world. Adolfo's pals were being named to important posts and Adolfo expected the same for himself.

Where would Party leaders put him? Would they make him leader of a province? Give him a major editorial post? Or would his work in Budapest lead him to the Ministry of Foreign Affairs?

When Joel Iglesias told him to see Aníbal, Adolfo filled up with a mixture of excitement and trepidation.

"Everything has been decided for you," the Party leader told him. "It is work appropriate for a priest: rehabilitation of counterrevolutionary minors who are in jail."

Counterrevolutionary minors in jail? Adolfo's testicles began to snore. Was this where his portentous beginnings and years of struggle had brought him?

With supreme difficulty Adolfo simply asked: "To whom do I report?"

"That's the way I like it!" Aníbal said with a smile.

At the Rebel Youth Adolfo's new posting received few comments. Some comrades got together for a low-key farewell.

Adolfo's buddy César was the only one to give an encouraging word: "They are preparing you for the Party's ideological work."

Adolfo was joining the Interior Ministry, an essential department in Castro's regime. One of Adolfo's buddies from the old Socialist Youth, Óscar Fernández, was the vice minister under whom he would work. Óscar gave him a warm welcome.

"We are moving the kids to a precinct jail in Marianao," [53] Óscar said. "That way it will be easier for you to work with them. Quite a few are still in with the grown-ups at La Cabaña and El Príncipe.[54] Finish moving them to the precinct jail and see what you can do. Those kids have set bombs! It's a mess."

"What are their class origins?" Adolfo asked.

"Nothing special – they're just ordinary boys who went over to the counterrevolution."

"Has anyone looked into their problems?"

"Around here no one looks into anything," Óscar said with derisive humor. "They make it up as they go along. And they don't want to hear about rehabilitation. They only think of jail or the wall."

"That's absurd," Adolfo said. "People become our enemies because of their interests. Why should people without property turn against socialism?"

"They just have – and at times to the death."

"They're confused," Adolfo asserted. "They're acting like cannon fodder. They have no business defending interests which aren't theirs."

"You can't underestimate the enemy's ideology." Óscar had turned completely serious. "For years imperialism has been

---

[53] A down-to-earth neighborhood in Havana
[54] Major prisons in Havana at which the regime's political enemies were being kept

indoctrinating people with anti-communist sentiment. Just remember, the ministry is always right – no matter what stories those boys tell you."

§§§

At home Galina's reaction was brutal. "It's incredible that they make you go into jails!"

"The rehabilitation of young people is a job that deserves to be done."

"Rehabilitation!" she said scornfully. "It's no kind of work for a man like you!"

"They didn't give me a choice."

"And you accept the Party's instructions just like that?"

"How is it possible that you don't understand a communist's position – you, being a Russian?"

"I understand it perfectly well! You can't count on leaders for anything. Why don't you stop concentrating on politics and study a technical subject? That way you can always have a career no matter what happens in politics."

"I don't care for technical subjects," Adolfo said disdainfully.

"You might care enough to get a telephone for this house!"

After much domestic discussion Adolfo had managed to procure a refrigerator from a friend in high office; but he and Galina still had no phone.

"Why do you torment both of us about this?" Adolfo asked.

"Because almost every other house we visit has one! Why not talk to one of your friends who can do something about it?"

"I don't like to use political channels for favors."

"Politics! Politics! The only thing that communists care for is politics, while in Moscow they don't even have a telephone book for the city. That's where your politics gets you!"

That tidbit of no phone book in Moscow surprised me. But I did not grasp the signal that had jumped in front of my nose regarding the enormous backwardness of the Soviet Union. As usual I tried to forget my personal problems by working.

At Marianao's precinct jail we found about 15 youngsters. I had brought four or five younger men from the ministry; we interviewed the prisoners one by one.

I underlined to my comrades the absolute necessity of all prisoners admitting their guilt. It wasn't to make criminals of them but to let them unload their past in a good, clean way and start fresh.

"What has been taken away from you?" I asked a prisoner called Toby.

"From me? Nothing."

"So why fight against communism?"

"Because I don't like it."

"Why?"

"Because it cancels my freedom. If I want to start a business, I can't."

"Do you think that if the government suppresses the lottery it is taking a hundred thousand dollars away from you?"

"No."

"How many people do you know who dream about getting the lottery prize? Many, right? And how many do you know who have actually gotten the prize? None, right?

"Listen up!" Adolfo said heartfully, man to man. "Juan Domínguez[55] has the same odds of starting a business and getting rich. Those are illusions! And you hold onto them to comfort yourself for the real things you lack."

"Not necessarily. My uncle is a Juan Domínguez and he made a business."

"He's an exception. People *do* get the lottery prize. But are you going to place all your hopes on that? Anyway, we don't bother people who make small businesses."[56]

Toby looked at me doubtfully but I kept up my argument. As I was absolutely sincere I didn't hesitate to agree with him when he made sense. My objective was to win the battle for that boy's conscience – to save him for the cause of truth and justice.

---

[55] John Doe
[56] That was soon to change.

43

Kissing a giraffe

Early 1960's. Adolfo and his brother were working for opposite ends. While Adolfo's job was to rehabilitate political prisoners, Emi's goal was to resist rehabilitation.

At first the Castro regime had housed common and political prisoners in mixed company. But then officials discovered that common criminals who came into contact with political offenders were speedily "won over to the counterrevolution." So political prisoners were kept in separate facilities, largest of which was on the Isle of Pines.

A far piece from the "Cuban Model Prison" it had been in earlier days, the Isle of Pines was now home to more than 4,000 persons crammed into four immense circulars, each holding about 1,100 prisoners awkwardly placed on six floors.

The top floors had not been built to board prisoners; but those in charge of Castro's penal economy, undeterred, put men there despite the fact that the corridors had no guard rails and men could easily fall to their death from that height. During prisoner counts, sixth-floor inmates had to stand on ledges with nothing but air behind them.

The first sensory impression in the circulars was of an overpowering stench. Prison engineers, in placing water pipes, had contrived to pass them through floor areas where prisoners' fecal matter was stored. Those pipes regularly overflowed, fragrant water cascaded down from floor to floor, and the expression "raining shit" gained a new meaning.

Together with that aroma, the strongest presence in the

atmosphere was the rehabilitation program. For most men rehabilitation smelled like a good deal. The obvious benefit was getting your sentence reduced. If you were not a criminal, the thought of even a few hours in jail was likely to be a burden. And many, perhaps most who landed in political prison were neither criminals nor even true enemies of the regime.

Multitudes of people in the circulars were those you could call "prisoners of chance." They had gotten arrested for casually saying things like, "The government is full of it" – as people with free spirits and clear consciences are everywhere given to do.

Under Castro's regime the consequences of such acts were not advertised, but they were heartbreaking. Reported by fellow citizens, arrested by State Security agents and put on trial, the offenders had drawn heavy, heavy sentences – 15 years, 20 years, even more.

Those innocents had cared little for politics and had taken no part in the conflict until they found themselves closed up inside Fidel's maw. They had no secrets to tell on themselves or others. They could apologize for their comments and recant without betraying their consciences. The aroma of rehabilitation could be sweet to them.

For hard-core resisters like Emi, rehabilitation stank worse than fecal water. And it was in their nostrils all the time, because the guards and the loudspeakers and the regime's agents in the prison didn't stop bringing it up. Rehabilitation was unthinkable to Castro's enemies because it proposed to turn them into Castro's allies.

For a start, that was dangerous. Many had chosen to resist Castro because they had seen how he treated his friends. And by embracing the regime they would not only have to betray their comrades; they would also renounce themselves.

One of the thousand-plus men in Circular Two was the same "Ernesto" onto whose farm Emi Rivero had parachuted during his final clandestine entrance into Cuba. Since Emi's questioners at the Special Interrogation Facility had mentioned the farm – "We can show you on a map where you parachuted" – Emi was not surprised to find Ernesto in jail.

Rather quickly Ernesto had established himself in prison as a dedicated enemy of the regime. He refused all efforts to get him to rehabilitate. He also showed coolness to Emi, who found the attitude surprising and disappointing.

Emi engaged the other man in conversation. As they stood at the rail on the circular's fifth floor, Ernesto talked about his own experience under interrogation.

"They tortured me with smoke," Ernesto said. "They made me smoke until I couldn't take it."

To Emi it sounded like an excuse.

How can one man make another man smoke? It's like saying, 'They made me stand on my feet.' No one can make you stand on your feet. You just fall down and make them hold you up. Making you smoke is even harder.

This man is lying. He chickened out. I thought it was one of his employees who told on us but it wasn't. It was Ernesto. He told on all the employees and he told on me.

Ernesto became a radical precisely because, after being captured, he had taken the so-called easy way out. As it happened, talking was no easy way out. Men like Ernesto, having talked, lost their morale; and Castro's people, having got the goods, only grew meaner to the men who had confessed. No wonder Ernesto was a big radical.

Castro's prison officials were a mixed lot. Some were idealists like Adolfo Rivero; others were sadists like many guards in the circulars. Whoever they were, their mission was the same: to gather information on "counterrevolutionary" activities.

Rehabilitation was not the regime's only means to this end. Security agents posing as inmates were everywhere, among the resisters and among the rehabilitated as well. Those agents became the prisoners' best friends, showing them affection, listening to their troubles, giving advice, encouraging them to talk, waiting for the fruits to drop – waiting months or years if need be.

At the same time, prison officials worked hard to intimidate and demoralize unreformed men. The "searches" were especially rough. All at once a guard cried out, *"¡Rechisa!"* – and a military detail, not the usual prison soldiers but some strange battalion of up to a hundred men, invaded the prisoners' quarters.

Every prisoner had a few seconds to grab up one or two things he could not afford to lose – eyeglasses, medicine, food – before leaving the cell naked, with his clothes in his hands. The men were kept away while the soldiers worked over their private spaces.

When the men came back they couldn't recognize their quarters. Mattresses had been ripped open. The little plastic bags with powdered milk, chocolate or coffee that you had received from your family had been torn apart. The floor was littered with foodstuffs. Books and magazines had been destroyed.

Communists of Adolfo Rivero's stripe were quick to assert that prisoners cannot make a difference because when people go into jail they lose their power. Adolfo's brother concerted himself directly against that idea.

In Emi's mind he was still at war. He didn't bemoan his fate. Castro's forces had caught him, put him on trial and locked him up in jail. Until they killed him, however, they could not take him out of the war.

Every day, with their every gesture, Castro's people in the prison made war on him. When they held up his mail it was war; when they kept him from sunlight it was war; when they gave him bad razors it was war; when they pushed rehabilitation it was the essence of war.

The first rule of war was to keep alive. How did one do that in jail? Emi's method was to stay active. From the moment he woke up at dawn or earlier to do his yoga positions, he made sure he had more than enough to do.

Unlike prisoners who slid into unkemptness, Emi shaved his face and head every day despite cutting himself. Every day he meticulously cleaned his living space. Every day he pressed his khaki uniform and wore it as if he were on display. He played chess. He taught judo and yoga. Above all, he read.

He was a wolf for books, hunting them everywhere. To his parents from whom he did not stop requesting books, he wrote: "This is my way of keeping prison from devouring me, as it has so many men."

He implored relatives in Cuba who visited him to bring books. Other prisoners lent him the books they had. Against all rules and customs he even got a prison guard to give him two novels, *Pitcairn's Island* and *L'Assommoir*.

Emi also took pains to acquire foreign-language study guides; he was training himself to read in different languages. After a time he was reading Dostoyevsky in Russian.

His encounter with German was formative. Only now could he appreciate the beauty of a language he had worshipped from afar.

His prison studies brought him back to familiar texts of Goethe and Nietzsche – writers whom he had studied in their Spanish-language vestments and who now stood forth as their undisguised selves. When at last he could speak to himself the lines of Goethe's that prefigured his high school romance with Lizbet, he nearly fainted from the beauty of the sounds.[57]

---

[57] "Elysium"{Gedicht} Johann Wolfgang von Goethe: Berliner Ausgabe. Poetische Werke [Band 1-16], Band 2, Berlin 1960 ff, S. 190-192.

Sie nähert sich mir.	She draws near to me –
Himmlische Lippe!	Heavenly lips! –
Und ich wanke, nahe mich,	and I quake at her approach,
Blicke, seufze, wanke –	gazing, sighing, trembling –
Seligkeit! Seligkeit!	Ecstasy! Ecstasy!
Eines Kußes Gefühl!	Bound up in a kiss!

When time came for lights out, Emi had worked and worked and still not finished his tasks.

To be a prisoner, he reckoned, was like kissing a giraffe. "Kiss me!" the creature said, and you ran up the neck. "Love me!" she said, and you ran down the neck. "Kiss me!" and up you went. "Love me!" and down you went. Up and down, up and down unto Infinity – and it was a life.

44

Topsy-turvy

1962. After working half a year for the rehabilitation of young people in prisons, Adolfo Rivero got some rehabilitation of his own from one of Cuba's political elders.

Fabio Grobart, a Polish-Jewish immigrant who spoke Yiddish better than Spanish, had helped organize the Cuban Communist Party/PSP in the 1920's.[58] Four decades later, Fabio was a senior leader who could look on Adolfo and experience a version of his former self.

He saw that prison work could not fulfill Adolfo or utilize his talents. Without noise he moved Adolfo into a writing job in the political theory department of the new governing organ, the ORI.[59] Thanks to that favor, Adolfo was back in the swing.

The intervening months had brought their share of sadness. Adolfo's disagreements with Galina had grown unbearable. He felt constantly undermined by her, while she felt he could not be a serious man. Separation was inevitable, and they took it.

Galina managed to stand quite well on her own. Her circle of Russian-language students kept growing, and in the burgeoning socialist state she built an enterprise – the very thing that Adolfo

---

[58] Miami publisher Kiko Arocha, who joined the revolutionary movement at Havana University in the 1950's, writes of Fabio Grobart that he "arrived in Cuba in 1924 sent by the Comintern and . . . was the true head of the communist party, which conveyed the Soviet designs." (note to the author, January 18, 2020)

[59] Integrated Revolutionary Organizations

had told his young counterrevolutionaries couldn't be done.

More trouble was coming. By early 1962 collectivist policies had cancelled Cuba's native prosperity.

After sustained attacks on private enterprise, the flight of Cuba's business class, war with the US and the end of Cuba's access to American markets, the nation's economy had cried uncle. Three years after coming to power, the best-endowed revolution of modern times introduced what it called a "supply book."[60]

By any other name, this was rationing.

Fidel announced the measure on March 12, describing it a temporary means to offset the economic effects of US "imperialism." In his talk Fidel held out a vision of "1970." Come 1970, he said, Cuba would have a fully functioning socialist economy that would be the envy of the world, surpassing the US itself in all indicators.[61]

March 13, the day after that announcement, was the fifth anniversary of the Directorio's attack on the Presidential Palace – a signal event in the anti-Batista struggle. A commemoration was to take place on the main staircase of Havana University. Fidel would deliver the closing speech, preceded by a student who would read from the testament of the uprising's martyred leader, José Antonio Echeverría.

When Fidel came forward, many imagined he would speak again about the rationing. Instead he launched into an invective over the fact that, in the reading from Echeverría's testament, all references to God and God's favor had been removed.

Fidel denounced the omissions as an act of cowardice. He

---

[60] Kiko Arocha, op cit.
[61] History would say otherwise. As of 2020 Cuba still had a ration economy – or, as the government's supporters might call it, a "supply economy."

thundered against "sectarianism" which, as he reminded his audience, Lenin had called "communism's infantile sickness." He portrayed himself as a tolerant, broad-minded leader. It was a spellbinding display, and his rapt listeners forgot all about "supply books."

Adolfo, attending as an ordinary spectator, was a tougher nut.

When has Fidel shown respect for the Directorio or its leaders? Since when has he cared for religious sentiment? How does it happen that not one of the country's leaders identifies as a Catholic, while only three years ago we all called ourselves Catholic?

Fernando Ravelo, Adolfo's old comrade at *Mella*, was now in charge of Rebel Youth at the university and had been one of the ceremony's organizers. As he told Adolfo, another leader had asked which fragments of Echeverría's testament should be used in the reading. Ravelo advised that since only a few lines were going to be read, those in which Echeverría asked for God's favor could be skipped.

So it had been a simple editorial choice – no censorship intended. Why then had Fidel made such a fuss?

A few days later Adolfo was preparing some materials for the youth magazine *Mella*, including a notice about the new secretariat of the ORI. In the list of leaders that came to him, a name had been crossed out. It looked like a typographical correction.

Adolfo had to dig up something in Fabio's office next door. Fabio was talking with the veteran Party secretary of Camagüey province, Felipe Torres Trujillo.[62] As usual "Felipón" greeted Adolfo warmly. Adolfo went about his business and vaguely heard the others talking about Aníbal. Back in his office, without

---

[62] http://www.adelante.cu/index.php/es/historia/61-personalidades/7187-felipe-torres-trujillo-modestia-revolucionaria-personificada

knowing why, Adolfo looked for Aníbal's name in the secretariat's list. It was the name that had been crossed out.

Adolfo felt as if a large, blunt object had smashed into his head.

When Fabio was alone again, Adolfo went to speak with him.

"Fabio, Aníbal's name is not in the leadership list. It is crossed out."

The old cadre looked at Adolfo and took a long pause. At last he said: "Aníbal is not in the leadership anymore."

"But that can't be!" Adolfo blurted, his eyes filling up with tears.

"Rivero," Fabio said in a weary voice, "after the criticism against Stalin, this is the heaviest blow I have received in my life." He paused again. "In revolutions we have disagreements, we have contradictions. Men make mistakes."

"Do you mean Aníbal made mistakes?"

The older man spoke with deliberation. "The crucial thing is that we have no divisions among us. We must keep the Party united under Fidel's leadership. The revolution marches on. Let us have no further comment about these issues."

Adolfo took the point. Aníbal, for whatever reason, had come into collision with the one man who had made communism a success in Cuba. To pick an argument with that man would endanger the whole achievement. No good communist would sanction it.

Unfair it certainly was. But then who should have felt for Aníbal more than Fabio himself? If Adolfo loved Aníbal as a father, Fabio loved him as a brother. The Party's main task – its only task – was to protect the revolution. Fabio was completely right.

Of course no limits applied to Fidel, who went on TV to talk about some "differences" in the revolution. Aníbal, or so the supreme leader said, had been a communist for many years – a good communist, an honest communist – but Aníbal had gone wrong. He had taken command of the ORI and made decisions that created chaos.

Actually Fidel had never lost or ceded control. He himself had been the bearer of the chaos. He was also disgruntled that Aníbal's power had become a check on his own. So he masked that resentment by turning it into a critique of Aníbal and the old communists, whom he accused of defending their sect – the Party – at the expense of the people's well-being.

At last the sense of Fidel's remarks about Echeverría had become clear. It was 'game on' in the war against sects.

The takedown of Aníbal was Fidel's first sally against the old communists. Since 1958 the Party had backed Fidel's *guerrilla* campaign with hardly a quibble. But now Fidel, instead of advancing the revolution, had simply eaten the Party stalwart who was blocking his way to total power.

The old-timers had not seen it coming. Their love of doctrine had blinded them to the danger of Fidel's *Realpolitik* – its utter lack of scruple. And they had badly misread Fidel, whom they had seen as a well-meaning youngster lifted to power by the logic of history.

A few years later, when the political moment gave Fidel another chance to show himself, the old-communist remnant would realize that their nice young *guerrilla* had turned out to be something more massive, more terrifying, and quite beyond their ability to control. But for now they could hold to the idea, beloved by communists everywhere, that they were moving with history and moving history themselves.

§§§

As the crisis of sectarianism unfolded, the First Congress of Rebel Youth was in session at the *Habana Libre*, the former Hilton Hotel. Adolfo decided to visit the sessions and found most of his old comrades turning their backs on him. César, his one remaining friend in the youth leadership, was getting the same treatment.

"They are kicking me out of the leadership!" César told Adolfo in a rage. "They are sending me to some out-of-the-way job – getting rid of me, just as they got rid of you!"

"Who got rid of me? When?" Adolfo said like a dotard looking for his eyeglasses.

"Wise up!" César exclaimed. "They took you out of the youth leadership because of your quarrel with *sectarianism*. That was thanks to Aníbal, the sectarian-in-chief! Wasn't it Aníbal who sidelined you in that work with prisoners? What kind of a job was that for you? Wasn't everyone surprised?"

At the time, actually, César had been the one to praise the assignment[63] – but that was César. Like Adolfo himself, he could argue one side of an issue and then take the other side just for fun. Very few people had that kind of braininess or humor. But Adolfo knew that in their friendship César was true-blue; and the present talk was a lightning-bolt.

Larger forces were working in César and Adolfo's favor. This time, ironically, their savior turned out to be the chief wrecking-ball of sectarianism: Fidel himself. In one of his talks Fidel called the Rebel Youth leaders "more Aníbalist than Aníbal" and kneecapped all of them with a good swift kick.

The leader's next move was to send his perennial sideman Raúl to the Youth Congress to "mediate" between Aníbal's men and César. Plainly the fix was in; César was acknowledged for his correct attitude and warmly reaffirmed as a youth leader.

---

[63] See Chapter 42, "Rehabilitation," above.

Having landed on top, César presented Adolfo's case and secured his return to power. Adolfo got the foreign relations portfolio of the Rebel Youth, becoming the international ambassador of Cuba's young people. When Fidel came to give the concluding address of the congress, Adolfo was up on the podium next to him.

45

The farm

{Adolfo's recollections}

1962. Shortly after its congress the Rebel Youth had been given a farm to turn into a model project. The farm, bordering the sea along the Matanzas highway, consisted almost entirely of rocky and sterile land.

Joel Iglesias – still director of the Rebel Youth, untouched by the purges – expressed serious doubts about the farm. I suggested forming a team of students from the faculties of agronomy and veterinary medicine to study the place and give an assessment regarding its possible use.

Shortly thereafter we met with the agronomy student who headed the group.

"That little farm is very bad," said Joel, who after all was a *guajiro* and knew rural life.

"Do you think it could be used for anything?" I asked.

"I think so," the agronomy student, a very likable and sharp mulatto, said earnestly. "We think it could be used as a study center of plant pathology."

"How do you mean?" I said, smiling inside because of where this was going.

"The problem is not limited to the lack of topsoil, or even to the fact that the reef is visible. We have detected several varieties of fungus and parasitical diseases. Lots of fumigation might clean the reef and put it in good shape – but in our view what's the point? It would be much better to get a good piece of land somewhere else. Then we would apply intensive techniques and we would get useful results."

Joel sighed. "The problem is that this is the farm Fidel gave us."

"That farm is not good!" the student put in. "I am ready to explain it to the *comandante*! We will sign a report with our names on it."

"No one can possibly disagree with this," I told Joel. "The country has so much good land that's crying out for proper care."

We agreed we would bring up the matter with Fidel.

At our next meeting Joel said: "Fidel, that little farm – we sent a team from the university to look at it. We had many students of agronomy, of veterinary medicine, and in their opinion the farm has no productive conditions whatsoever."

"One does not have to pay too much attention to technicians," Fidel asserted, smiling mischievously to Emilio Aragonés[64] who smiled in turn.

Joel objected. "The place is bad –"

"When I was told it was bad," Fidel broke in, "I said, I'm going to give it to the young, and you'll see how they will make it produce."

"But *comandante*," Joel insisted, "I don't know what we are going to do! It has no topsoil!"

"Why haven't you brought topsoil from the Zapata swamp?" Fidel asked. "You could have brought it in trucks."

---

[64] A member of Castro's inner circle

To carry mud from the Zapata swamp 200 miles away and build up an artificial soil on the reefs – how much would such an operation cost? What meaning could it have? Hadn't the government just explained the country's serious situation regarding fuel? Wasn't gas being rationed?

We remained silent as Fidel spoke about the swamp and the crocodile farm he intended to organize there. "Crocodile hides have a very good price in the international market," he affirmed. "By 1970 we will be exporting them in substantial quantities."

There it was again, "1970"– the date by which big transformations would be achieved. Indeed they would, but not in quite the way people expected.

46

Under the mushroom

{from Adolfo's recollections}

Rebel Youth headquarters, Tuesday morning, October 23, 1962. Adolfo sat writing at a large conference table when the door opened and four or five comrades entered. Joel Iglesias, who walked with a slight limp, came striding toward him.

"Hi Joel. What's up?"

"Haven't you heard the news?" Joel asked with urgency.

"No, I've just arrived."

"Last night Kennedy declared a naval blockade on Cuba."

"A blockade! What does it mean?"

"It means no ships will be allowed to enter Cuban waters."

"No ships? But what sorts of ships?"

"No ships, dammit! None!" Joel was dead serious.

"What about oil?"

"No ships – no oil, no food, *nothing*. Get it?"

"It's the real thing, Adolfo," César chimed in.

"But – but – the Soviet Union cannot let its ships be stopped in mid-water!" Adolfo sputtered. "That would be war!"

"Good! You see?" César said to Joel. "He's smart. You just have to give him a little time."

"Let's meet tonight after I hear from the Party," Joel said. "Most probably I'll stay in Havana and you guys will go to the provinces."

That night, outside the building, they said goodbye to each other.

"See you under the mushroom!" Adolfo's buddy Carlos Quintela said, going to his car.

"Bullshit! Everyone loves his own skin," another departing comrade said, putting down Quintela's nonchalance.

"What the hell! See you under the mushroom," César said, leaving.

Adolfo climbed into his car. His driver Bebo was at the wheel.

"Home?" Bebo asked.

"Yeah. Tomorrow we leave for Santa Clara. *If.*"

"Good for you!" Bebo said. "In Santa Clara you can see that girl you like."

Next day in Santa Clara, as danger continued to hang over everyone, Adolfo took charge of the local youth organization to deal with the crisis.

Late in the evening Bebo drove him out of town to an old house with a tiled roof. Adolfo knocked on the door. No one answered.

"Are you sure it's here?" Adolfo asked his driver.

"Yeah! This is the address."

"Who is it?" a female voice asked from inside.

"Good evening!" Adolfo said. "Is Marisa there?"

"Yes, right here! I was in bed. I need a minute."

"No hurry!"

Marisa emerged in her militia uniform. The sight of the beautiful 17-year-old gave Adolfo all the encouragement he needed.

"Hi!" she said, giving Adolfo a light kiss. "How's the situation?"

"At least Nikita and Kennedy are exchanging letters. But it's a strange feeling. And I decided to give you a present the next time I saw you."

He reached in his pocket and brought out a small box, handing it to the girl.

"It's not a fine ring but it is my mother's." Adolfo had reclaimed the ring from Galina when they broke up.

Marisa was astonished. "I had never thought of marrying so soon!"

"Yes," Adolfo said, "but the situation is that we are revolutionaries and we have made a socialist revolution in the face of the strongest capitalist nation in the world. We cannot expect them to forget us. And we cannot expect to live normal lives."

"Of course," the girl said haltingly.

"We might be blown up at any moment."

"Aren't you exaggerating?"

"Listen," he said intently. "Have they made a naval blockade against Cuba or not? Is the possibility of an atomic strike real or not?"

"They have. It is."

"And here we are," he said, kissing her passionately.

47

Rōnin

Sunday, October 28, 1962 and following. Six days after
Kennedy's announcement of a naval blockade, the missile crisis
abruptly ended when the Soviets agreed to remove their nuclear
weapons from Cuba.

Fidel had no part in the agreement, which he had to learn about
from news reports. Quite bitter, he skulked away from the Soviet
alliance; for the next six years, until he again accepted Moscow's
embrace, he had no clear bearings in the wider world.

For Emi Rivero and thousands of his fellow inmates, the end of
the crisis was a heartbreaking affair because it spelled the death of
any chance that Castro might be overthrown by the US.

For Adolfo and his buddies, on the other hand, life began anew.
Their outfit had yet another name. The Rebel Youth, which for
years had been called the Socialist Youth, now became what it
had always wanted to be: the Communist Youth. With gusto
the young communists went back to the ordinary pleasures of
political destruction.

Adolfo's buddy César, in addition to holding a place in the youth
leadership, headed the Union of Cuban Pioneers, the organization
of schoolboys. In Adolfo's eyes it wasn't much of a job but César
loved it.

That kind of situation was typical of power in communist
structures. A typesetter at the regime's daily newspaper might also
be a member of the Party leadership and would have more clout
in political matters than the newspaper's editors. In the same way,
César's humble job with the Union of Pioneers didn't reflect his
bigger influence as a youth cadre.

When the position of youth leader for the Havana district opened up, César put in for the job and the Communist Youth directors gave him their backing.

Surprisingly, however, the Party's Havana district said no. The order came from the new general secretary for the capital region – Joel Domenech.

Him again! How had he survived the purges? Besides being the toughest of sectarians, Domenech had also been Aníbal's "man at the side of Fidel." With Aníbal purged from power and disgraced for his association with "sects," Aníbal's man ought to have been a memory. Instead he was bigger than ever.

It had to be a piece of unseen craft. While no one was looking, Domenech had stopped being Aníbal's man at the side of Fidel and had become Fidel's man at the side of Aníbal.

César and Adolfo did not make the connection because they were too sincere for their own good. When Domenech put forward his own man for the post of youth leader in Havana, César and Adolfo challenged the others to a debate in front of Cuba's president, Osvaldo Dorticós.

Adolfo, predictably, complained about Domenech's behavior in the argument over Rolando Cubela. Domenech, acting in character, called Adolfo's assertion a lie. As the debate quickened, Fidel strutted into the president's office.

Not seeing that they had been outplayed, Adolfo and César only grew more animated. Fidel trained his fury on them and hollered with the loudest voice in human history: "You don't have faith in me, and I don't have faith in you!"

After a few moments Fidel calmed down and said he couldn't be happier with Adolfo and César. But he was speaking softly to men whom he had just laid waste.

The youth leader post went to Domenech's man, Isidoro Malmierca. Some time later, at his pleasure, Domenech moved César and Adolfo out of the youth organizations.

The victors had big futures in the hierarchy,[65] while Fidel's thrashing had given Adolfo and César a clear vision of their destiny: to be *rōnin*, samurai without employment.

For now were let down gently. Raúl Castro took César for the military academy, while Adolfo received a pair of academic posts: a chair in philosophy at the newly formed Schools of the Party, and a professorship in Marxism at Havana University.

In a letter informing his parents of the changes, Adolfo struck a wistful tone. "One cannot have everything in life, and every road taken brings satisfactions as well as renunciations."

Not yet out of his twenties, Adolfo had started to sound autumnal.

---

[65] Domenech would become minister of industry; Malmierca had a 15-year run as foreign minister.

48

Companionship

{Emi's recollections}

Isle of Pines, 1960's. In prison we had some men with us who, without being political offenders, had committed crimes beyond the ordinary. We called those people *fronterizos*, frontiersmen.

The frontiersman I knew had gone to prison for his role in assassinating a well-known person from an elite family. The crime had occurred during an earlier period when Batista directly or indirectly ruled the country.[66]

One day I was giving a judo lesson to a fellow inmate on how to do a stranglehold. As the other man was trying the hold with me as his dummy, the *fronterizo* passed by and told my student: "Hey! Careful with the doctor!"

Everyone froze, including other prisoners who were watching. They were afraid the *fronterizo* might kill the man for putting a hand on me. The frontiersman had an air of violence about him and seemed to carry, under his clothes, a prison-made knife.

Prisoners avoided his gaze for fear he might draw the wrong conclusion. Food servers – violent criminals who fed the political prisoners – avoided speaking to him. The guards allowed him to leave his *galera* – a privilege they denied other prisoners – because he liked to clean the walkways, and even the guards preferred not to bother him.

---

[66] The Paniagua family; the earlier period of Batista's ascendancy was between 1933 and 1944.

The frontiersman cleaned my cell every day. Whatever I was doing, or with whomever I might be speaking, he came to the cell, threw water on the floor without saying a word and started mopping.

He also brought me tea. Among Cubans who universally prefer coffee, my tea-drinking habit was so rare that when I was in the underground I wondered whether police might track me by asking in the cafés about who came for tea. In prison the frontiersman served it to me every day. At a given moment he shouted at the top of his lungs for everyone to hear: *"¡Doctor Rivero! ¡Té!"*

No one understood why the man paid me those attentions. It's true I used to give him my monthly allotment of cigarettes, which in prison was a treasure; but I think that wouldn't have persuaded him. I believe he responded to me simply because I treated him with *compañerismo* – comradeship, respect, and a touch of affection.

No one else at the Isle of Pines extended him that courtesy. Then again, I've never followed the crowd.

49

Renato

Isle of Pines, 1964-65. For the first time in three years of imprisonment, Emi and his fellow *plantados* – "staunch ones," militants, political offenders who refused any form of rehabilitation – were being allowed to sit and walk in the sun. Their feelings were indeed euphoric. But they might have reflected that they were not getting the gift for free.

Indeed the regime was preparing another surprise – a change that only governments like itself could perform. It was planning to erase a category of citizens from the national community. But first the targeted group would have a walk in the sun; while the regime's leaders could present themselves as decent fellows before quietly burying a group of 'society offenders who might well be underground, and who never would be missed.'

The political prisoners identified fully with their status. If not for their political or moral scruples they would never have come to the 'big jail.' Most had not been in trouble with the law for more than a traffic ticket. Distinct from the blue fatigues of common prisoners, their khaki uniforms defined them and gave sense to their lives.

In the summer of 1964 prison authorities were preparing to draft inmates for work on nearby state farms. The work orders contravened a long-standing custom in Cuba and elsewhere that people in jail for political offenses may not be forced to do manual labor. But the Castro regime, having plunged the island into a rationing system, had now taken things to another level of chaos.

As a result, many extra hands were being recruited into various forms of "voluntary" labor which was not really voluntary.

The issue raised uncomfortable issues of revolutionary justice. To see political inmates reading literature, talking of Greece and Rome, sitting in the sun and consuming the people's food, while the rest of the country worked hard to eat, really didn't sit right.

To remove the prohibition against drafted labor – and here was Fidel's novel idea – one need only cancel the category of political prisoner. That could be done simply by taking away the khaki uniform. Get rid of the uniform and, *voilà*, a new work force.

The tactic was pregnant with a kind of violence that unitary regimes adored; it eroded human souls in a way that hardly anyone else might notice or measure. But first in the regime's order of priorities was to extract labor; canceling the khaki uniform was the cherry in the *parfait*.

New work orders came down gingerly, a piece at a time. Late on a summer's afternoon Emi and his fellows caught sight of a brigade from another circular on its way back from outdoor work. It was a horrible sight; the men looked so utterly worn down and dejected.

A phrase from Cervantes popped into Emi's mind: *«Gente forzada del rey, que va a las galeras»*[67] – Men condemned by the King, marching to the galleys.

"To hell with it!" Emi decided. "I'm not doing that!"

He talked with a number of pals including Alfredo Izaguirre. Those two had come a long way since the day that Emi – as Brand, trying to steal away from Cuba after Plinio's execution – had sought help from Alfredo and Alfredo had withheld it.[68] After parachuting back into Cuba, Emi had enjoyed the full measure of Alfredo's comradeship; and when, some months after

---

[67] https://cvc.cervantes.es/literatura/clasicos/quijote/edicion/parte1/cap22/default.htm
[68] See Chapter 23, "A jog to Key West," above.

his own arrest, Emi learned that Alfredo had been picked up in a counterintelligence sting, he had been deeply upset.

At the Isle of Pines Emi and Alfredo made a potent combination. As Alfredo was some ten years his junior, Emi affectionately called him by the diminutive 'Alfredito.' The younger man was just as determined to resist the new orders.

"Sign me up! I'm not going to work either," Alfredito said.

"How can we create a scandal over this thing?" Emi wondered. "You belong to some kind of world press association, don't you?"

"The International Society of Newspaper Editors."

"Why don't you get yourself beaten up? That would make a scandal for sure."

"It's not a bad idea!" Alfredito said.

Alfredito picked a fight with the guards. They gave him the beating of his life; he almost died. But no scandal resulted, and within days Alfredito was listed on the work detail for the circular.

For refusing work, Emi and Alfredito were taken from the circular and placed in the "punishment pavilion," a separate facility where inmates who broke the prison rules were kept in solitary cells.

The punishment pavilion was an extended one-story structure with several rows of cells fanning out from an entranceway. Each cell was just large enough for a man to take one or two steps inside. A window made of concrete blinds admitted air but no light.

The cells had different doors; some had barred windows that admitted light from the corridor, while others were iron slabs that let in pinhole-sized beams of light for just a few moments each day. To keep from having your eyesight destroyed by dark, you had to station yourself in front of that beam and let the light, for those few moments, bring your eyes to life again.

In every cell the ceiling was low, a permeable roof letting in rain. By day you broiled from heat while at night you shivered, since minimal food rations did not allow you to generate the caloric energy that would keep you from feeling cold.

Bed was the floor or, in special cases, a canvas sling. Food came in through a hole in the door. Toilet facilities were a hole in the floor and two faucets, an upper and a lower.

The guards had to turn those faucets on and off, one cell at a time. As they hated this duty and hated the prisoners, the guards enjoyed playing games with the faucets; as a daily ration, the prisoner was lucky to get two aluminum dishes of water before the guard stopped dispensing it.

Each prisoner had only a pair of underdrawers and a pair of aluminum dishes. All other possessions – books, magazines, cards, games, writing supplies, pillows, bedrolls, foods, parcels that your loved ones might have sent you – were forbidden. So were all communications with the rest of the world.

For the entire time that you were "on holiday" in the pavilion, you did not see another human being; but prisoners could talk between cells by raising their voices. When one man was talking to another several cells distant, the men in the intervening cells piped down as a courtesy.

In Miami, Emi's parents realized something had gone very wrong when they stopped receiving his letters. One of those to whom they turned for help was Adolfo, who took the side of the regime.

In a letter of February 1965, Adolfo told his parents that the disciplinary measures against Emi were not life-threatening and were an appropriate response to his disobedience. As Adolfo wrote: "In a prison it's not the prisoners who give the orders."

{from Emi's narrative}

In the pavilion we were constantly being moved around from one cell to another. By mid-1965 Alfredito and I were in the same corridor, our cells not far apart. We used to play chess. We played blind, announcing our moves to each other, since we had no paper, pencil or any material that could be used as board and pieces. We considered that this practice would greatly improve our game if we were ever again to play chess in the normal world.

It was during those days that Renato and I met.

He was a toad about an inch and a quarter long. One morning, waking up, I saw him perched on the edge of one of the two aluminum plates that I always kept full of water.

I took care in moving around the cell so as not to harm or frighten him. Apparently he was a calm individual, self-assured, for even when I sat on the floor near him, observing him intently, he kept cool and detached, outwardly above any passion that might move a toad.

In order to give him some bearings and authenticity in our fractured world, I named him Renato. I told my fellow prisoners about him. When I got food I always left some drops or grains in case Renato might want some – though I never saw him eating any.

As days went by and Renato stayed in the cell, I didn't realize what a comfort his company had become. How could I? How could the mood of a rational being – of a man hardened through civil strife – be buoyed by the casual presence of one of the humblest of creatures; and one who didn't establish a rapport with men?

One morning I awoke and found he was no longer in the cell. More than two decades later I still feel the sadness with which I told Alfredito, "Renato is gone."

50

How long shall the wicked . . .

{Emi's recollections}

Isle of Pines, March 1966. After a year and a half in the punishment pavilion, Alfredito and I had become a kind of tourist attraction. Whenever G-2 officers came from Havana to inspect the penitentiary, they were taken to the pavilion where they walked along the corridors, at times stopping at the barred doors and asking questions of prisoners.

I got used to the fact that they always stopped at my cell, and that the officer guiding the visitors introduced me with the phrase: "This one is the shit of the prison." On leaving, many of the officers told me: "You are going to rot in there."

My usual reaction was to smile or laugh – which infuriated them, for they took it as an act of bravado. In fact it was nothing of the sort; it's just that I have a sense of humor.

Around this time I heard something outside my cell that astonished me. It was a woman's voice. My heart jumped so violently that, weak as I was, I almost fainted. Of course it was natural, this tremendous love of man for woman, and its absence had made all of us ill.

At one time Alfredito and I had been the only inmates to have stayed in the pavilion for more than a month. By now however two others – Odilo Alonso, a Spaniard, and Nerín Sánchez , an ex-Rebel Army officer – had joined us as permanent guests.

The lack of light and a decent diet had caused all of us to turn skeletal. I had lost my eyelashes and eyebrows. We were living as less than animals. Rats and insects, passing by, looked over their shoulders at us.

The four of us decided to begin a hunger strike, demanding decent food, vitamins, the right to be outdoors three times a week, and the right to send and receive letters. Until our petitions were granted, we would accept no food from our jailers.

As soon as we had stopped accepting food, the pavilion became even gloomier and more ominous than before. Prisoners talked in lowered voices and more rarely. Almost no one spoke to us, apparently for fear of reprisal by the guards.

At dusk the first day of the strike, my friend Gregorio Ariosa called out to me. I approached my cell's barred door.

"Rivero, I imagine what you are going through. I hope your problem is resolved soon. I know this is the worst time of the day for you. I also know you are not a believer. But I know you like the Bible. So every day at dusk I will recite from the Bible for an hour."

It was Ariosa who chose what he was going to recite. When I heard a verse I especially liked, I asked him to repeat it. Sometimes I asked several days afterward. Whenever I asked, he recited it to me again without the slightest hesitation; and the beauty of those verses became a balm for me.

"O Lord God, to whom vengeance belongeth, show thyself. Lift up thyself, thou judge of the earth; render a reward to the proud. Lord, How long shall the wicked, how long shall the wicked triumph? . . ." [69]

"The Lord reigneth; let the people tremble: he sitteth between the cherubim, let the earth be moved. The Lord is great in Zion; and he is high above all the people. Let them praise thy great and terrible name, for it is holy . . ." [70]

The hunger strike went on for days and more days. Many times

---

[69] Psalm 94
[70] Psalm 99

I listened to Ariosa while lying on the floor, for I felt dizzy and feared that if I stood too long by the bars in the door, I would faint and injure myself in a fall.

I developed a strong liking for Hebrews XI and a preference for some of its verses: "By faith he sojourned in the land of promise, as in a strange country . . ." "By faith the walls of Jericho fell down, after they were compassed about seven days . . ." And also The Acts XXVI: "And as he thus spake for himself, Festus said with a loud voice, Paul, thou art beside thyself; much learning doth make thee mad. But he said, I am not mad, most noble Festus; but speak forth the words of truth and sobriety . . ." "Then Agrippa said unto Paul, Almost thou persuadest me to be a Christian . . ."

On the 17th day of the strike we were promised by the garrison officers that our petitions were going to be granted. We started eating again; but after a week, when we saw that their promises had been a ruse to test and break us, we started the strike again. Through it all, Ariosa didn't stop his recitals – not once, no matter how the guards threatened us or how foul-tempered they became.

One evening Ariosa kept talking with me after he had ended his recital. We spoke, as we often did, about the United States. He enjoyed listening to my stories about the States which he constantly interrupted with questions – his intense longing for knowledge. On that particular evening I heard his voice breaking and quivering.

"Is it true that in the United States they throw dogs at the black people?" he asked.

I felt my throat close. Tears came to my eyes. This man looked at the United States, dreamed of the United States, as a promised land – yet he was black, and a terrible doubt burned in his mind.

"Yes," I answered, "it's true. The United States has minorities that are racist and look with hatred at the black people. But you know, Ariosa, the majority of white Americans look with even greater hatred at the white racists, for they understand that the racists contradict and corrode the ideals that make the United States great."

I hoped that some day I could prove my point to him.[71]

§§§

After 20 days of their second hunger strike, the four protesting inmates were removed to the prison's medical facility; the regime was not prepared to let them die. One by one the men were lashed hand and feet to hospital beds and fed through the nose.

As Emi was brought into the sick-room and saw his friend Alfredito tied to a bed, he mustered all his strength and aimed a blow at the collarbone of the officer who was about to tie him up.

The blow was respectably hard, coming from a man who had scarcely eaten in 40 days, but the guard was merely stunned. Emi was then strapped to a bed and force-fed along with the rest.

After 18 days of being fed that way, the four inmates were strong enough to be transferred. The Isle of Pines community – one of the world's largest concentrations of political prisoners – was being disassembled because it had become a liability to its overlords.

The body of political inmates had broken the regime's effort to cancel their identity via the imposition of work brigades. They had committed large-scale sabotage against the work projects, doing poor jobs and burying their tools where guards couldn't find them. Inmates caught at sabotage had been beaten and confined to the pavilion; but prison authorities could not force the body of men to serve as Castro's oxen.

---

[71] Ariosa did reach the US, where he recorded a YouTube video about his prison years; https://www.youtube.com/watch?v=wOeJNgzX6pQ (Spanish only).

Adolfo Rivero's memorable assertion to his parents turned out to be memorably incorrect. At the Isle of Pines prison, it was finally the prisoners and not their jailers who gave the decisive orders.[72]

---

[72] The former model prison is today, in the poet Shelley's phrase, a "colossal wreck." For a visual, see http://strangeabandonedplaces.com/the-strange-abandoned-model-prison-of-cuba/

51

Closer to the race

1966, prisoner migrations. After managing with his fellow inmates to close the political prison at the Isle of Pines, Emi Rivero was transferred to Havana's La Cabaña fortress, a stone monster whose countenance had grown even more severe since the trials and executions that had ushered in the Castro regime.

The prisoners at La Cabaña had greeted Emi as a celebrity – a notion that did not sit well with him. The guards had a similar reaction to the inmates who had famously refused the common prisoner's uniform. As one of the guards told Emi about Alfredito and himself: "You guys f—ed around a lot in the Isle of Pines, and we are keeping you in our sights." [73]

La Cabaña was the fresh new ground on which the same pair of armies kept up their battle. Guards took away the khaki uniforms and replaced them with blue fatigues, which dissenting prisoners refused to wear. Those men were left in their underdrawers and confined to their cells with no time outdoors.

Feelings in the prison ran dangerously high. Anxious to resolve the dispute, Interior Ministry officials sent a man to speak with the prisoners. The meeting, while cordial, failed to find a resolution.

Shortly after arriving at La Cabaña, Emi had been summoned to a visit. Emaciated from the hunger strikes, he went to the visitors'

---

[73] Alfredo Izaguirre Rivas, 1938-2014 https://www.thecubanhistory.com/2014/06/a-goodbye-to-alfredo-izaguirre-rivas-photos-un-adios-para-alfredito-izaguirre-fotos/

room in a sheet slung over him like a toga. At the rendezvous he found his first wife Lizbet, whom he had not seen since the day of their separation more than a decade earlier.

In the intervening years Lizbet had remarried and divorced. Apart from her son Emilito who was now almost 20, she had no man in her life. Her father, whom Emi adored, had recently died; while her brother had been killed in the invasion as a member of the anti-Castro brigade.

Lizbet wanted some tie to a man and she felt compassion for Emi. So she took care of him in jail, visiting regularly.

It was the kind of tribute that validates a man's life. The mere thought of her, standing outside the prison under a hot sun with a bag of goods she had prepared for him, touched his heart and brought him closer to the human race.

52

Haunted house

Cuba, mid-1960's. "Nothing here is going the way it should!"

"Yeah, Fidel is stubborn. He thinks he can succeed with a policy he calls Marxism. But he's watching the wrong movie."

"Really? Which movie is that?"

"Man and Michelangelo in Cuba."

"Never heard of it."

"It hasn't yet been made."

"So how can Fidel be watching it?"

"Fidel does things no one else can do."

"And he expects the rest of us to rise to his level?"

"We are revolutionaries! We have a duty to be exceptional."

"What if we are just ordinary?"

"We have to change."

"What if we can't?"

"In that case, Fidel will get a new people."

"Impossible!"

"I told you! He does things . . ."

"Okay, okay! What are we supposed to be doing today?"

"Today we are producing."

"Producing what?"

"We still haven't heard."

"You mean the bosses themselves don't know?"

"They are waiting to hear from Fidel."

"Maybe we should just give speeches."

"That's Fidel's department."

"What about strategies for production?"

"Fidel is in charge of strategy."

"Doesn't he have enough to do?"

"Forget it, buddy! We are riding that famous forefinger all the way to the moon."

Who in Castro's realm would have been talking this way? Prisoners? Asylum inmates? Ghosts?

Actually they were Adolfo's gang, still serving as officials in the regime.

In 1965 Fidel re-minted the Communist Party as *his* Party. No longer was the revolutionary coalition a hodge-podge of entities with names constantly changing. From now on the only valid name was 'Communist,' and the only leader was Fidel.

Cuba's new Communist Party had come to life with the conceit that its revolution was a starting-point of humanity. The fresh-faced *fidelistas* were ignoring Soviet history, among other things.

In Adolfo Rivero's phrase, the Party adopted a platform of "socialist deconstruction." [74] Official procedures of all kinds were abruptly cancelled. Accounting was abolished. Fiscal measures were used for foreign exchange only. Cubans continued to receive salaries and spend money, but no economic system was present to back up the exchanges.

The state lowered to a few cents the cost of many public services – home telephones, buses, mass transit, cinemas and other spectacles. Certain services, like the use of public telephones and admission to sporting events, were officially declared free of charge and remained so for lengthy periods.[75]

Adolfo and his friends – young men and women who had succeeded to the mantle of "old communists" – were deeply principled people whose views had years of ideological training and habits of careful scrutiny to back them up. They were aware that utopian experiments of the kind being instituted by Castro and Ché Guevara had been attempted by the early Bolsheviks – with disastrous results.

The new "old communists" kept up their support of the revolution. They also considered themselves obliged to speak out against policies that could bring harm to society.

In their view, to smile and keep one's mouth shut while the country went rolling downhill was bad behavior. They fought hard on the ideological front, even as they kept losing influence with higher-ups who told them: "You're too strident. When are

---

[74] Deconstruction wasn't a social program. But if a daredevil in the domain of ideas had used it as a blueprint for society, the outcome could have looked like the mandated chaos that Castro produced in Cuba during the middle 1960's.
[75] According to Adolfo and others who lived in Cuba during the 1960's and 70's

you going to grow up?" Or at other times: "You're too grown-up."

Adolfo and his buddies heard themselves described by other officials as "pro-Soviet." In context it was an ominous term. Ironically, though, it was at about this time that Adolfo and his friends began rethinking the Soviet experience.

In 1966 and 1967 the writings of Isaac Deutscher, with their novel viewpoints about the Soviet Union, were enjoying a vogue among intellectuals in Cuba and elsewhere. Deutscher, a Polish communist living in Britain, had some years earlier published epic biographies of Trotsky and Stalin. Those narratives had shown that the immense cruelties of the Stalin period were not merely unfortunate byproducts of Soviet Russia's progress, as Nikita and others had claimed. Rather, as Deutscher told it, Stalin's governing style was the essence of a system corrupt at its heart.

That view of the Soviet system had come not from an ideological rival but from a sympathetic participant of deep and searching intelligence. Furthermore, it was delivered in a compelling narrative style. The impact of Deutscher's books in Cuba, as the revolution became the product of a single man's fantasies, was especially striking.

Reading Deutscher, Adolfo and his buddies felt betrayed by everything they thought they knew. In answer to Castro's nonsensical utopias, what did sincere communists have to offer if not the "realism" of the Soviet experience?

Adding to the sensation of Deutscher, a pair of Polish communists had mounted a remarkable challenge from within Poland itself. Jacek Kuron'and Karol Modzelewski, exact contemporaries of Adolfo's, had published a unique statement of dissent: a 95-page "Open Letter to the Party" [76] The pair had been quickly arrested, and the news of their dissent ran like quicksilver across the communist world.

---

[76] https://www.marxists.org/history/etol/newspape/isj/1967/no028/kuron.htm

Adolfo and his friends were feeling strangely mortal. They had started to sense that their pleasing abode – their neat and shapely ideology – was actually a haunted house of history. And from within their own house they were hearing bizarre, terrible screams.

53

A very healthy climate

1966-68. In late 1966 Brian Pollitt,[77] son of British communist leader Harry Pollitt, came to Cuba to do a study of rural peasants – a favorite Cuba project of the time for trendy intellectuals on the European Left. In Havana the Schools of the Party set up a sociology team under Adolfo's direction to support the study.

The researchers were looking at peasants in the Escambray. It was a tough subject. The people of that central region had put up a massive armed resistance against Castro; many thousands had had to endure forced relocation by Castro's armies who were 'cleaning' the region of all communities that might aid the rebellion. The *campesinos* who remained, when scholars came to talk to them, were chary in what they said.[78]

It was nonetheless an interesting, stimulating project. Adolfo's wife Marisa had agreed to leave her studies and come along. She and Adolfo spent months living on top of a mountain. Each day they wore themselves out in trekking. Marisa didn't mind the rough conditions at all. She loved the hikes and put on pounds climbing the mountains.

At night, when they turned off the light in their shack, a tremendous noise broke out. What was it? They turned on the light; rats were scurrying all over the room. Marisa couldn't have cared less. She had fantastic toughness and stamina; the harder things got, the better she became.

---

[77] https://grahamstevenson.me.uk/2011/07/17/pollitt-brian/
[78] For a present-day introduction to the theme, see Enrique Encinosa, *Unvanquished* (Pureplay Press, 2004), Chapter VI et seq.

Only, something was missing between them. Adolfo felt it even
if he couldn't explain it. Marisa was a good companion, a good
comrade; but here they were, two young people on a mountain,
with nothing and no one in the way, nothing to keep them from
getting close, and they did not get close.

§§§

Late in 1967 Adolfo left for a sociology conference in Évian,
France. His friend César, seeing him off at the airport, asked
enigmatically: "Why don't you think about staying there?"

César had an uncanny feel for political developments. Adolfo gave
it a thought but took no action.

Had he changed his plans, he would have saved himself quite a
bit of trouble.

Like his brother on the day of his capture, Adolfo was standing at
a fork in the road. As with his brother, the road he chose was the
hard one.

People of conscience are often drawn to the more challenging
path, which gives at least one advantage: it lets you see precisely
where you stand. To Adolfo as to Emi, the hard road gave another
advantage: it paid back a personal richness that either man would
have missed on the easy road.

The price you pay on the hard road is obvious. The price you pay
by ducking obstacles and taking the easy way out is much tougher
to reckon – and is frequently not less grave.

§§§

{from Adolfo's recollections}

Weeks after returning from Europe, I was still processing data
from the Escambray study. Such rote-work was completely boring
to me, though fortunately Marisa took care of things with her
usual efficiency.

On that day late in January we went to have lunch, as always, at the Schools of the Party dining room. After lunch we were engaged in table talk when my close friend Félix de la Uz showed up, looking worried.

"Let's beat it," Félix told me. We took off on his motorcycle.

What was happening? Félix was strangely silent.

At last he turned his head and told me: "Your name is included in a report that is going to be published in *Granma*. You are named as a member of Aníbal Escalante's faction."

I felt my face and hands turn cold.

"But I have not seen Aníbal in more than a year!" I cried back at Félix, hardly able to hear my own voice.

The thing made no sense at all. César had come and said to me: "Look, Aníbal just sits around his house all day with nothing to do. Why don't we drop in?"

Where was the harm? It was a chance to talk to history. If Churchill or De Gaulle were sitting on a porch reading a newspaper, who in the world would not go and speak with him?

At the Schools of the Party building we climbed up to the top-floor office of our boss, Leonel de Soto. The room wasn't very big but it was carpeted and air-conditioned. Leonel received us with his usual smile.

"Things are bad," he said.

The Central Committee was in session and had broken for lunch. Leonel, a member, had used the break to return to his office and send Félix for me.

Leonel told us that Raúl Castro had presented a report alleging a new scheme on Aníbal's part. "They call it a 'microfaction.' Your name appears at the very beginning of the report, together with César's. He is mentioned again but not you."

I guessed that Leonel, with his last comment, was trying to console me. As a rule, however, one shot to the head is enough.

"What does the report say?" Félix asked Leonel.

"That Aníbal does not agree with anything."

Félix launched into an explanation of how absurd it was to lump me in with Aníbal. He spoke with his usual passion and clarity. Leonel sat listening attentively. But this talk between them was only a gesture of solidarity – of sympathy.

"I told you not to visit Aníbal!" Leonel said to me when Félix was done. "I even gave you a message from Fidel!"

"And I heeded that message!" I answered, exasperated. "Even before you talked to me, Carlos Rafael[79] had mentioned it, and that was enough for me not to visit Aníbal again!"

"You should never have gone in the first place. A lot of people from the old Party are involved in this mess," Leonel said. "Aníbal resented the anti-sectarian campaign. And he still has ambitions. He was meeting with people at the Soviet embassy."

"It's another purge!" I said bitterly.

"If Fidel were not distrustful, he wouldn't be alive," Leonel answered.

It was obvious. Anyone disagreeing with the report would look like part of the conspiracy. So everyone would agree.

---

[79] Carlos Rafael Rodríguez was a 20th-century communist leader who might be called Cuba's Talleyrand. He served in Batista's wartime cabinet and went on to serve Castro for nearly 40 years.

Leonel stood up. "I have to go back," he said, pressing my shoulder with affection. "Perhaps they won't publish the report."

Félix rode me back to the cafeteria, where Marisa was waiting. As we walked, I had to give her the news.

"Perhaps it will not be published," I concluded.

"Let's hope so," she said desolately.

Of course it was published.[80] Headlines blared out the accusations as facts:

Conspiracy of the microfaction!

Conspiratorial activities!

How and where the traitors met!

Approaches to foreign governments!

Insidious labors of trickery and proselytizing!

Clandestine circulation of statements against the revolution!

The report went on and on with eye-witness accounts, official commentaries – acres of words running over into the next day's newspaper, which it also filled.

The day of the first installment I went to have lunch as usual at the Schools of the Party. No one came to sit with me. Only one man stopped and said: "You are radioactive."

The image struck home. I decided not to return there so as to save my colleagues from further contamination.

---

[80] *Granma*, January 29-30, 1968

The day of the second installment, Félix invited me to the Centro Vasco restaurant with Javier de Varona and Ezequiel. Those were friends; they were courting professional failure and public censure of the most putrid kind.

Javier raised a glass. "To Siberia! They say it has a very healthy climate."

54

Zarathustra

A short time after the microfaction report, Adolfo and Javier de Varona, along with Félix de la Uz and Ezequiel, produced a lengthy statement on Cuba's governance that ran to 80 pages.

Adolfo's buddies knew of the Polish "Open Letter to the Party" and almost surely had it in mind when they came to write their manifesto.[81] Unlike the Polish dissenters, they politely submitted their work to authorities via official channels. Notwithstanding, the Cuban statement was tough and clear in substance.

Its main point, in Adolfo's words, was that "Cuba's problems derived from an incorrect application of basically fair principles . . . It was [Castro's] personality and his political 'deviations' that hindered economic and social development, not the communist conceptions in themselves." [82]

In the summer of 1968, Kiko Arocha – an engineer and disaffected ex-communist – answered a knock at his door. It was Adolfo, whom he had not seen in years. Their acquaintance dated back to the anti-Batista struggle at Havana University. They also shared a trusted friend in César Gómez.

Adolfo handed Kiko a fat wad of paper. "Have a look and tell

---

[81] See Chapter 52, "Haunted House," above. In a message to this writer, Kiko Arocha said: "It seems to me . . . that the inspirers of our Cuban friends were the young Poles who in 1964 wrote 'An Open Letter to the Party.'" (email of January 25, 2020)

[82] From notes that Adolfo shared with this writer

me what you think," he said without ceremony. "I'll come back tomorrow."

Next day, when Adolfo returned, Kiko said with enthusiasm: "It's awe-inspiring! The whole story is there. The only thing is, I don't like that final paragraph."

The conclusion stated that only Fidel could make things right, and that Fidel remained Cuba's legitimate leader. "How can you say that the source of all our problems is the one who will fix them?" Kiko asked.

"We are giving this to the Party," Adolfo said. "We need that statement to keep them from destroying us. In case they try, we've sent the statement outside the country."

Kiko made several copies. He gave them to trusted colleagues at the National Center for Scientific Research. He also gave a copy to his assistant, whom he hardly knew.

The assistant snitched to police.

Kiko was arrested and interrogated at Security headquarters. He took an uncooperative stance. Authorities kept him at Security for 62 days and then shipped him to a labor camp on the Isle of Pines without bringing charges or giving him a trial.

The infamous political prison had already been closed by a prisoners' revolt against forced labor.[83] But the regime was still collecting people in that locale to use as beasts of burden; and Kiko was put to work there as a slave.

After fourteen months they told him he was 'free' to return home. For the next three decades, Kiko "lived as a third-class citizen in my own country."

---

[83] See Chapter 50, "How long shall the wicked . . . ," above.

§§§

To this day the document that put Kiko into a labor camp remains unknown. Kiko discarded his copy, as apparently did Félix. A short time after the group had submitted it to the Party, Javier died mysteriously.[84] Adolfo kept his copy; but twelve years later, during a raid on his apartment, police found the wad of paper and confiscated it.[85]

As of this writing, Ezequiel – who lives with his wife in Havana – is the only survivor of the group that created the paper. If he doesn't have a copy, then the only ones in Cuba with access to it are the archivists of State Security and the Communist Party.

After half a century, it's time for that paper to come out of the shadows. To give the statement a clear identity, the author of the present work is calling it «Zarathustra». Like Nietzsche and his prophet whom Adolfo admired, this Cuban Zarathustra bears a message for people everywhere.

The Castro line of rulers may be expected to keep Zarathustra in a drawer. But that fate can be overturned by an individual. Will someone in Cuba or elsewhere, having access to the document, open the drawer, set it free, and let it find its way to the audiences it deserves?

---

[84] Kiko Arocha to the author, April 2020
[85] See Chapter 63, "A city on crutches," below.

55

Proletarians

1968-69. At the end of May 1968 Adolfo wrote to his parents about his plight and that of his friends, thrown out of their jobs for supposed ideological offenses.

"We continue without work even though they keep paying us. I have no idea what I'll be able to do. I've run almost half the course of my life and still haven't managed to cast anchor.

"My only security is in the principles that have directed my life and in the affections of a close few. It's very curious for me, nonetheless, that certain general experiences have a wide range of validity. Among my friends, for example, certain of Dad's sayings which I constantly use have become very popular; also, to be sure, some of Emi's.

"I still think I was right in the fundamental areas. But things were infinitely more complicated than I had thought."

Seven months later, at the beginning of 1969, Adolfo told his parents: "With the end of the year, the long process of my discussions with the Party also came to a close. Actually I took part in just two meetings, one in June and one in October, the second one only to receive the Party's statement, which took five minutes.

"I was told that I had 'serious differences with the Revolution,' that the Party was 'breaking relations' with me and that the Labor Ministry would determine my work situation . . . I am only permitted to work as a field hand or in a factory. Among possible options which the comrades at the Ministry discussed very gently with me, we came to the conclusion that 'electrician's assistant' would be best.

"So this year will find me changed into a proletarian – one of those whom I have dedicated my life to defending."

Part Four

Victories

<u>56</u>

Chivalry

1969-70. After more than eight years in the Cuban prison system, Emi Rivero still had not consented to the regime's proposal that he relinquish his identity as a political detainee.

In 1969 Emi was abruptly transferred from La Cabaña fortress to the Castillo del Príncipe, another Havana prison, where he spent just a few weeks before being transferred again to Guanajay prison, some thirty miles outside Havana.

Not only did the dispute over uniforms remain. A more sensitive deprivation was in store. At Guanajay the guards confiscated his personal possessions, including his books.

Despite his resolve not to show rudeness to guards whatever they did to him, Emi went into a fury over the seizure of his books. He raised his voice to his captors and yelled: "The only way to coerce me is for Fidel Castro to come here and suck my prick!" [86]

Screaming like an inmate of Bedlam, he added: "If snitches are listening, you can repeat what I say to your friends in the central administration!"

To talk that way in the depths of Castro's prisons was not bravado. It was insanity. The books were returned. Even so, Emi regretted his loss of control.

---

[86] *"¡La única forma que hay de coaccionarme a mí es que Fidel Castro venga aquí y me mame la pinga!"*

{Emi's recollections}

Though my section in Guanajay prison was not having visits that day, the guard called my name and said I should be prepared to leave the cell "correctly dressed." I assumed my family had managed to get an extra visit.

As I looked around for one of my relatives, the guard told me to follow him. We went through the hall to the prison's entrance. A Security officer was waiting for me. He signed a paper and signaled me into a car where two guards waited.

The Oldsmobile took off for Havana in a great hurry; the speedometer showed between 160 and 180 kilometers per hour. The driver was quite good.

We arrived at State Security headquarters. I was led through stairwells and corridors to an upper floor. An officer came out of a tiny reception room and told me I was about to see Dr. Guillermo Alonso Pujol.

I immediately recognized the man who had served as Cuba's vice president under Carlos Prío. Now living in Venezuela, he had kept up a strong interest in Cuban matters and was in frequent contact with my parents, whose friend he had remained.

"For almost two years I have been working for your freedom," Dr. Pujol said. "Your father is gravely ill. I beg of you: Do all in your power so that this effort of mine on your behalf will bear fruit. Don't make me fail."

"I am being asked to discuss things I know nothing about, or things I cannot talk about," I replied. "And they are asking me to wear a common prisoner's uniform, which is something I can't accept."

The Security officer who had been watching our conversation intervened.

"You must wear the uniform the Ministry has chosen for you," the officer said. "Presently you are in a state of rebellion and we will not consider freeing you unless you change your attitude. As to your activities, we know all about you. There are just a few details that you must tell us. If you fulfill those two conditions, we will consider releasing you."

Dr. Pujol looked at me and said: "I have presented your case at the highest levels of the Cuban government. The persons with whom I have spoken want to be certain that you are not going to engage in activities against the state if you are freed."

I answered: "My only interest is to go back to my family and reconstruct my life. As to politics, the Cuban case is over for me."

"Would you be willing to say that in writing?" Dr. Pujol asked.

"I have no objections."

As I wrote the letter I told Dr. Pujol of my doubts that State Security would be convinced by it. They would insist on my giving information, and as a consequence we would have no deal.

"What importance do you attribute to talking about things that happened nine years ago?" Dr. Pujol asked. "That belongs to history. Do not jeopardize the opportunity I have of giving you back to your parents!"

"Apparently these gentlemen want to turn me into an informer, and that is something I don't accept."

The officer again interjected. "No one is trying to make you an informer!" he insisted.

The meeting ended in a stalemate.

§§§

In trying to secure his release, Emi's parents were working parallel to the CIA whose main interest was to protect their intelligence nets from being disclosed. American officials were purchasing the release of their agents from Cuba with hard cash.

From allusions in his mother's letters, Emi understood that his case was a subject of negotiation between the CIA and Cuban authorities. But he had no idea that CIA negotiators were displeased with him for refusing to take an "easy" way out.

When CIA officials talked to Emi's mother about their failure to make a deal in his case, they were full of rancor. "Your son wants to stay in prison!" they told her.

"No, that's not true," *la vieja* said firmly. "What he wants is not to be a traitor."

57

Destiny

Guanajay prison, October 24, 1970. « *Wilkommen, Bruder!* »
Welcome, brother!

The greeting, belted out *fortissimo* and in a strange language, astonished the many inmates, visitors and guards who could not avoid hearing it. Emi and Adolfo were seeing each other for the first time since their contentious lunch in Havana a decade before.

This meeting had originated with *el viejo* who called Adolfo from a Miami hospital. When the old man implored him to visit his brother, Adolfo took the request for a dying father's wish.

It was a duty Adolfo reviled and feared. For him to be seen with his brother would be a gross political discredit. He no longer had the privilege of working in politics – but in Cuba everything was political and he needed the job he had. How would his bosses feel about his going to visit an imprisoned CIA agent?

Anyway, here they were, together for the first time in ten years.

Emi went straight to it. "Listen! Have you read Isaac Deutscher's volumes on Trotsky and Stalin? They are extraordinary works!"

Given the vogue that Deutscher's books had gained in Cuba, Adolfo was not surprised that Emi should have seen them. But the news that Emi shared his language in this crucial matter was a lightning-bolt. At a stroke, Emi had come close to his heart.[87]

---

[87] For Adolfo's view of Deutscher's work, see Chapter 52, "Haunted House," above.

Adolfo grew animated and lit a cigar. He gave Emi his account of the microfaction episode, of his expulsion from the Party, and of «Zarathustra», the 80-page statement written by him and other comrades.[88] Emi, for his part, was fully aware of the campaign that Fidel's regime had waged against his brother and listened sympathetically.

"What about an early release?" Adolfo asked.

"I'm not optimistic," Emi said, mentioning the talk with former Vice President Pujol.

"I agree," Adolfo said. "The thing is, you are trying to get out of here clean – and they do not want to let you out of here clean."

Emi gave a look which his brother could read very well.

"Just think about it, will you?" Adolfo said. "You don't have to *be* broken. You just have to *look* broken. You have to give them something."

§§§

I said goodbye, took my cap and went out of the prison. I left and he stayed. It was shattering. What moved me was that I had behaved so badly toward him and that he had taken it all so well. The ride back to Havana was very difficult. A friend was driving me. I did not want to break down in the car. When I got home I didn't even greet Marisa. I just blew past her, went straight to my room and closed the door.

---

[88] See Chapter 54, above.

<u>58</u>

Laurel & Hardy

Havana, 1970's. In the midst of Adolfo's loneliness, almost as an afterthought, Marisa conceived; and in May 1971 Alejandro was born.

From that date onward Adolfo's letters talked of almost nothing but an infant in peach-colored skin. In 1975 he told his parents:

Alejandro was in Marisa's lap and I said to him; 'What you like best is to play, right?' Marisa, teasing, said to him: 'What would you say about your papi? What does papi like best?' He said: 'To read and drink rum.' I said to him, 'That's pretty good. You're a smarty pants. How about your mami? What does she like best?' He thought it over and said: 'Oh, nothing special, just being here like this with me.'"

In his phrase, Adolfo was living through "grey years" whose only redeeming value was the love of a peach-colored boy. As it happened, that one value – taken with a bit of rum – was quite enough to point the way to happiness.

§§§

Adolfo and César had met at Havana University during the underground movement against Batista. They quickly grew inseparable. A mutual friend, Kiko Arocha, said that in their closeness they reminded him of Laurel & Hardy. The observation gives rise to a piquant thought: how would Laurel & Hardy have played in a Cuban Communist setting?

When the University of Havana reopened in 1960,[89] the Party
appointed César secretary general of its youth movement there.
It was a prestigious assignment.[90] The Party considered the
university to be "the seventh province of Cuba,"[91] due to the
enormous influence of the student union – a quarry of future
politicians, members of congress, ministers and presidents.

César was a political prodigy, with an ironclad talent for logic that
could crush any opponent in a debate. When he spoke at meetings,
he seemed to be delivering the word of God. After he had spoken,
people behaved as if nothing else remained to be said.

From 1962 onward, the circle of César and his wife Thais
included many communists who, like themselves, were disaffected
by Fidel's policies. César's enormous talent should have made him
a cabinet minister or more. But he spoke without checking the
party line, and his frankness consigned him to marginal positions
in the highly regimented Castro state.

Like Adolfo, César suffered a complete disgrace when Raúl's
report named him as part of the microfaction conspiracy.[92] But
the two friends reacted differently. Around 1975 Adolfo asked
César for a private talk. César knew what was coming, and he
feared it.

They met on a beach in Havana and swam far away from shore,
to a spot where no microphone could pick up their exchange.

---

[89] The university had closed on orders of the student union in 1956 so that
student militants could dedicate themselves to Batista's overthrow; see Chapter
5, "Winds of change," above.
[90] See Chapter 26, "Revolutionary democracy," above; notably, the importance
that the communists gave in their debates to anything that touched on the
university.
[91] That phrase was told to the writer by Kiko Arocha. In 1960 Cuba was still
divided into six provinces: Pinar del Río, La Habana, Matanzas, Las Villas,
Camagüey, and Oriente.
[92] See Chapter 53, "A very healthy climate," above.

Even then, César kept splashing the water to make a wall of noise that would frustrate any recording.

Adolfo said: "I have decided to break with this regime."

"You need to be careful about that," César cautioned.

"I'm done being careful. I intend to make this open and public."

"Please don't!" César implored. "Those people are sons of bitches and they will kill you!"

"I will not let my actions be ruled by fear," Adolfo said firmly.

"But they will destroy you in such a way that you will not want to live!" César said with an aching heart. "And besides, I will have to break with you in order to protect myself and my family." Along with Thais, he had a daughter and son to consider.

"I know," Adolfo said, coming close to his friend's tone. "That's why I'm here – to say goodbye."

Laurel & Hardy would never meet again.

As time deepened, César grew increasingly self-protective and fearful. He removed himself from politics. He finished his degree in chemical engineering and took an ordinary bureaucrat's job. He and Thais divorced. Both remarried.

In the mid-1980s Kiko ran into César on a city bus. When they were passing near a park, César whispered: "Let's get off."

Kiko was titillated; he thought they would spend a few minutes playing around with politics as they had in the old days. But when they took their seats on a park bench, César launched into a tirade *pro* Fidel.

The leader, he said, was being attacked by sinister political forces from here or there. It was a strange outburst, coming from someone who had no resemblance to Kiko's old friend. Here instead, it seemed, was a guy from one of the neighborhood 'block committees.'[93]

Kiko was astonished. He could only listen in silence.

A decade later Kiko went into exile. A score of years after that – 2014 – César passed away in Cuba.

For Adolfo the loss of that friendship was a doleful melody that played *sotto voce*, right up to his final hours. But even as he lost his tie to César, Adolfo had made his most vital discovery as a man. Alejandro, the peach-colored dot of a boy, was actually a vast reservoir into which Adolfo could pour all the sweetness and all the tenderness that his parents had given him.

---

[93] Also called "Defense Committees," the neighborhood spy groups are Cuba's principal means to enforce a single idea: that every citizen's loyalty belongs first and last to the revolutionary regime.

59

The love that belongs to you

Combinado del Este, Havana, April 1978. Emi was
approaching the end of his second decade in Fidel Castro's special
accommodations for wayward citizens when he received a letter
whose arrival was the last stage of a very long pursuit.

Who would be pursuing him? It seemed to be his daughter. But
how could Ermi be pursuing him, or anyone?

She couldn't. Three-year-old Ermi was gone, and 19-year-old
Irma Alicia was standing in her place.

Through childhood and girlhood, Irma Alicia had a void at the
center of her life: no father. The man, or so she was told, had
died long ago in the fight for Cuba. He was painted a martyr,
paid homage in hushed tones on solemn occasions, and otherwise
forgotten.

If Irma Alicia and her brother had known their paternal
grandparents, who actually were living close by in Miami, it
would have been different. But those grandparents could not get
anywhere near the children.

Los viejos knew perfectly well that they had grandchildren near
them. From time to time, using his reporter's skills, *el viejo* was
able to ascertain that the kids were fine. But the elder Riveros
were powerless to affect their separation from the children.

Irma Alicia's brother Rubén, blond and beautiful, was his mother's
sweetheart; he gave no apparent thought to his father. She, on
the other hand, was a rebel. She rejected the reality that her
elders were feeding her. As a teen she snuck around in closets and

drawers, hunting for clues about her father – trying to sniff his blood.

At age 19 she found an item in Miami's Spanish-language press that described her father as he actually was: a well-known counterrevolutionary serving a 30-year term as Castro's prisoner. She contacted the reporter and asked for her dad's address. It was the Combinado del Este prison in Havana.

In a letter dated "Valley of the Fallen, April 19, 1978," Emi told his daughter: "Whenever I thought of you two – and not a day went by that I didn't think of you – nostalgia would cast a shadow over my recollections. But now your lines are here and everything is changed. Now, at a stroke, my children are beside me. I have been expecting your letter, because I have lived secure in the knowledge that sooner or later you would come in search of the love that belongs to you – a love that no circumstance of life can take away."

60

A kick in the pants

1970's. The people who made Cuba's socialist revolution, Adolfo and his friends prominent among them, thought in terms of power, not rights. They embraced the communist idea of class war, of one group in society against another. Such a war would go on until all memories, all echoes, all traces of the other side had been destroyed.

It was not a war across recognized boundaries. It was a war that raged inside society, inside a neighborhood, inside the family house. It became a war of one bedroom against another – even, at times, a war between people who slept in the same bed.

Finally it was a war inside each person. People were estranged not only from each other but also from themselves. And so the generations of Cubans would henceforth be made.

Cuba's leaders had pronounced Adolfo Rivero a counterrevolutionary. Adolfo despised that judgment but did not resist its consequences. Even as an outcast, he held so strongly to the idea of the revolution that he accepted its most vital claim: its power and therefore its right to make a mess of his life.

Eleven years went by before someone shattered Adolfo's idea that he must live as an outcast. How had it happened? Who had broken the back of his defeatism?

Had it been his father, the one he loved most in this world? No, *el viejo* had died in Miami in 1975 bereft of his home and sons, whom he had not seen during his final fifteen years.

Had it been his elder brother, the puffed-up personality who had loomed over his life for so long and who even now, from the distant reaches of Castro's prisons, continued to exercise a hold on him? No, it had not been Emi either. Much as Adolfo had come to admire his brother, Emi was still a specter to him, not quite a living being.

How about Marisa? Not likely. While she and Adolfo had found an accommodation, she was still married to the revolution. They could live in the same house and they could share a son, but they were not playing for the same team.

Surely then it must have been his buddies, the intellectual cream of the young communists. They had gone together through the big events; they had known the revolution inside out. Like Adolfo, those fervid young people had been disgorged by the beast and had come to experience the revolution from outside in.

They got together on weekend afternoons for a bottle of rum and a chat about the things they knew best. More than any others *they* were Adolfo's people, the ones who had strength and meaning with him. If anyone had been able to change his mind, it must have been his buddies. Mustn't it?

No, had it not been his buddies either.

Late in 1978 the American government under President Jimmy Carter began a process to reinstate its ties to Cuba, broken some 17 years before. As a consequence Castro decided for the first time in all those years to allow visits from the Cuban migrant community in the United States.

One of the first to get a visa was Adolfo's mom. After the family's separation, the wrenching disputes, Emi's capture and imprisonment, his own disgrace and demission, and finally the death of *el viejo*, this impending visit by his mother filled Adolfo with dread.

January 1979. Adolfo met his *vieja* in the lobby of her hotel, the *Habana Libre* – the old Hilton. Despite her years and life she was still young and beautiful, while he felt green and timid as a boy. Alejandro, his own seven-year-old boy, was with him.

As they stood on her terrace in a lovely winter breeze – Adolfo's favorite weather, grey and gusty – *la vieja* turned to him and said: "How long are you going to let them kick you in the pants?"[94]

There and then his intention took shape. Soon after *la vieja's* visit, Adolfo picked himself up from his secure, unhappy life and raised his face to the unknown. He went to his inner sanctum and typed out a note in which he asked the authorities for a visa – the right to leave the country.

---

[94] "*¿Hasta cuándo permites que te den patadas?*"

61

Full circle

Combinado del Este, Havana, 1979. Even more than opening
the island to visitors from the Cuban-American community, a
dramatic effect of the Carter-Castro diplomacy was that Cuba
started giving early releases to political prisoners.

Among the prisoners designated for release were journalists.
Emi Rivero was in that group, thanks to his Havana University
diploma and thanks more to his cover story, the one he had given
at his capture and kept up for 18 years.

When Emi saw his mother for the first time since his trial –
touched by her youthfulness, only noting a raspiness in her
voice – *la vieja* told him: "Make no mistake. You are going to be
released."

As 1979 went on, political detainees were being let out of the
huge Combinado del Este prison at the rate of 100 or 200 per
month. Emi understood his case would be difficult. Even if the
regime felt cornered into acknowledging him as a journalist, he
knew his captors were under no illusions.

What he didn't know, and couldn't yet know, was how decisively
he had beaten them.

In September 1979 Emi was summoned for an interview with
a G-2 officer. "In case the government has to release you," the
officer told him, "we don't want to be forced to execute you first."

Castro's minions were not well advised to bluster to men like Emi
and Adolfo. That threat of execution merely showed how weak
the regime felt itself regarding Emi's imprisonment.

The plain fact was that Emi had worn his captors out. In 18 years of confinement he had given them nothing; and he had shown himself ready to finish his term doing the same. He might die at their hands, but in death he would leave them no more than a sack of trouble. They would be smarter to use the diplomatic opening as a cover for losing him.

Another issue intervened. Apart from his family in the States, Emi also had a family in Cuba – his first wife Lizbet and their son Emilito. Their prison visits had become a mainstay of his. He well knew their desire to leave. He petitioned the authorities to let them go out with him.

Emilito was a talented engineer. The authorities didn't want to lose him, too.

"If you do not let them leave," Emi told his jailers nice and level, "I will not be able to put the Cuban case behind me because I will be thinking about them here."

That was the incentive they needed. They issued passports for all three. Regarding Emi's release, the official statement merely noted with a touch of pomp that Cuba had "no further use for the prisoner."

In October 1979 Adolfo was able to tell his mother: "As I write these lines he has already been out a week. He's almost forgotten his prison life; he's not a man to live looking backward.

"He's in extremely good form, physical and mental . . . What's unavoidable, of course, is that he's somewhat disconnected from reality. He's like a diver coming out of water; he needs time to decompress . . .

". . . Someone has to put into his head the notion that he is lacking in wickedness – or what used to be called 'contact with reality.' He needs a bit of healthy mistrust. As a reader, as a student, he has the experience of a sage. He is also finely honed as a warrior. But as a man of the street? In this respect he has less experience than his years . . .

"With his children he must not expect miracles. He will be dropping like a parachutist onto grown people who have made their lives without him. He will need tact and patience . . .

"He and I have talked plenty but of course not enough. A few hours of conversation cannot fill the vacuum of so many years. The surprising thing is how well we understand each other. In a way I'm not surprised. The experiences we've lived are different but complementary. I think that we are and will be essential for each other – irreplaceable – wherever life happens to take each one of us."

§§§

At a moment during the eight days he stayed in Havana between exiting prison and leaving the island, Emi went into a "dollar store" and bought himself a watch. It was a pleasing accessory, and Adolfo took notice.

"What's that watch?" he asked.

"A watch," Emi said absently.

"Yes, but what brand?"

"I don't know."

"Brands are important!" Adolfo exclaimed.

"Why?"

"They have a moral importance! They signify the right to choose!" Adolfo was full of emotion.

Their discussion of a quarter-century before had come full circle.[95]

---

[95] See Chapter 3, "We need a revolution," above.

62

Sophistication

October 1979. After flying from Cuba to Costa Rica and then to Miami to see his family, Emi went to Washington DC, the city in which he would live.

His goal in the US capital was to work with policymakers who dealt with Cuban matters – especially those who concerned themselves with Cuba's activities in Latin America. Cuba was working as an adjunct of the Soviet empire throughout Latin America and even in some countries of Africa. Emi could help the US in those matters while keeping his word to apply no force against Castro's regime.

His first stop was the CIA in whose interests he had labored for nearly 20 years. The people with whom he had worked would be gone, but their successors would be waiting to see him.

First he was examined by a government doctor who couldn't believe his instruments. Emi did not measure up like a man who had spent nearly twenty years in Castro's dungeons. At 51 he was youthful and physically fit, with a bounding vitality.

When Emi asked about his debriefing, a young CIA staffer informed him that no debriefing would take place. Not to worry, the young man assured him; the CIA would issue a payment to cover all his years of back service, which came to a tidy sum.

To Emi it was old wine in a Coca-Cola bottle. Echoes from his early days with the agency went rushing between his temples. *Americans throw money at difficult situations. As long as they give you money, they think they own you.*

As in 1960 money was not the first of Emi concerns. His aim was to assist the US policy process; he wanted to put his knowledge and experience to their best possible use. The bad news facing him – very bad news – was that the people in Washington who had known him best would not be giving him that chance. They were buying him out.

The young staffer was ready with explanations. President Carter was in the process of re-making relations with Castro. This reform would have major benefits for the US, for Cuba, and for the hemisphere. America's activities from the early 1960's were now part of a discredited past. Any remnant of that old policy would stop up the works if it reappeared now.

Adolfo especially, in years to come, would have a riposte for that kind of argument: *I guess it's what you would call sophistication.*

63

A city on crutches

{from Adolfo Rivero's recollections}

Havana, April 4-5, 1980

For years I had not been able to walk across the city's neighborhoods without being struck by their decayed, sordid, ruinous appearance – display windows that were empty and full of dust, nailed-up doorways, faded wall posters, plaster scaling off the walls, broken sidewalks. In the middle of the city, vacant lots unexpectedly appeared – the mark of recent demolitions. Everywhere the eye went, people had placed wood beams to prop up their crumbling door frames and balconies in an effort to forestall the demolitions that were coming. It was a city on crutches.

In the midst of this chaos, a store called "The Cinnamon Tree" – *El Canelo* – was a haven of structure, clarity and faith. It had also been the site of Adolfo's kills in the used-book trade. That afternoon he made a haul: a collection of essays published by Harvard University, a biography of Hannibal, an antique edition of comic stories. He took the books home, starting to look them over in earnest. Seeing it was 4:30, he went out again to find Alejandro who would be walking home from school.

Ale came along right on schedule, his eight-year-old body keeling over to one side with the weight of his book bag. As always, Adolfo went forward to snatch the case and take his boy's hand for the brief walk home. Leaving Ale to his amusements, Adolfo rejoined his new companions on the terrace, wondering whether he should start with Hannibal or with Ruskin's discourse on flowers.

A car came to a stop in front of the house. Marisa was home from the bureau. In a moment she was on the terrace. "Why don't we go to the movies?" she asked.

Adolfo's first thought was to stay home with his books. But then he took in her cool, direct tone and understood: Let's not have another boring Friday night at home.

"Sure. Why not?"

They went to the Teatro-Cine Trianón, noted these days for the good condition of its air-cooling system. The feature movies were a pair of American confections that Ale liked well enough. When they came out of the theater a sea of people was waiting to get in. The buses were crowded, too many people queued up for them, so they went home on foot – a 40-minute walk, Ale protesting all the way.

En route Adolfo picked up a copy of *Granma*, the official newspaper. A front-page item announced that Cuba's police guards had been withdrawn from the embassy of Peru. A group of six people, trying to enter the embassy grounds where they planned to seek asylum, had crashed a bus into the embassy's fence. In the ensuing fracas, a Cuban officer had died.[96] Cuba asked Peru to hand back the refugees for trial on murder charges. Peru chose to honor the tradition of asylum venerated in Latin countries.

In *Granma* the government defended its removal of the police guard by saying: "We cannot protect embassies that do not cooperate in their own protection." [97] But Cuba's response had been a highly aggressive counter; the regime was opening Peru's

---

[96] Kiko Arocha writes: "The assailants were unarmed. One of the guards shot at them and killed another guard by mistake. The government made believe" that the fugitives had done the killing. (note to the author, January 18, 2020)
[97] "Havana Removes Guard From Peruvian Embassy," *The New York Times*, April 5, 1980

territory to vandals, toughs and other troublemakers.

At home Adolfo took a bath, watched a bit of TV and went to bed on his library sofa. He awoke to the sound of violent knocking on the door. He got up, went to the door and cracked it.

"Police! Open immediately!" someone shouted into his face.

Dazed and wearing only his underdrawers, he let them in.

"Get dressed and wake up everyone in the house! Don't touch anything!" a gray-haired mulatto, obviously the senior officer, directed him.

It was six. Adolfo went back to Marisa's room. She was already up and dressed. Ale, who slept in his mother's room, had not awakened in the commotion. Adolfo let him sleep.

"It's the police," he told Marisa. "They're just looking the place over. Don't be frightened."

He put on some clothes and went back to the vestibule. Now that he could focus, he saw five men: the mulatto and another man in uniform, a plainclothesman, and two of his own neighbors, directors of the Revolutionary Defense Committee for the block.

The senior officer brought out a paper, looked it over and told Adolfo: "You are accused of having stolen artworks in your possession. The members of your Defense Committee are present to verify this accusation."

"All these paintings are mine," Adolfo said.

"You have receipts for them?"

"No one gives receipts for paintings. I've had most of them for years. I think I can find the former owners."

The police went straight for Adolfo's room. As they realized how many books, periodicals and papers were packed in there, they visibly lost heart.

"This is unbelievable," the senior officer said with a heavy sigh.

They began taking books off the shelves, inspecting them one by one. "Hey! This one has an official seal in it!" the other uniform, a beefy young white guy, exclaimed.

"Okay," the senior officer said, "that means it's stolen."

"It means nothing of the kind," Adolfo said with a rising voice. "You know as well as I do that the revolution, *for many years now*, has been closing up libraries and selling off the books. I've got dozens of books with official seals in them."

"This is a diary, isn't it?" the plainclothesman said, picking up a notebook.

"It's just a miscellany – notes, random ideas, brainstorming . . ."

The plainclothesman read out: "'True atheism resides in indifference. May we not say, on the other hand, that the passionate love atheists project toward mankind is actually a *religious* feeling?'"

The senior officer turned to Adolfo and said scornfully: "You're looking for a lot of things, aren't you. You're looking for art. You're looking for God. You're looking for a way out of the country. Doesn't it occur to you that you might be looking for too much?"

Those lines had the unmistakable ring of State Security.

"I can't help that," Adolfo answered. "It's my character. It's why I became a revolutionary."

"You've changed a lot."

"Yes. I've never seen inertia as a virtue."

After two hours' exertion the police had disassembled the library. They opened the bathroom closet – and their faces dropped to the floor as they found it even more densely crammed with books than the other room had been.

They rifled through the closet haplessly. In one of their probes they came across a rather fat document that looked unlike anything else. The senior officer leafed through it and picked up his head in alarm.

"The commander-in-chief is mentioned in here!"

"It's an old memo that was sent to the Party leadership," Adolfo said in his best matter-of-fact tone.

In fact it was much more potent. This was «Zarathustra», the 80-page statement he had written with Javier de Varona and others during the microfaction episode.[98] Just now he did not want anyone in authority to be reminded of it.

The officer set aside the document like a sapper handling a live mine.

When they had done with Adolfo's materials, they had little else to inspect. Looking in the bedroom closet, one of them turned to Marisa and asked: "These are all the clothes you have?"

"Yes. It's not much, is it?" she said sadly.

"Your husband has to come with us," the senior officer told Marisa. "We hope this gets cleared up soon."

The police took a few dozen books and a stack of papers, including Zarathustra. They withdrew to give the couple a private moment. Adolfo and Marisa sat down on the bed.

---

[98] See Chapter 54, "Zarathustra," above.

"Listen, *vieja*," he told her, trying to sum up everything in a few seconds. "Just remember: Life is a game. Don't give too much importance to any one thing. And *please* don't suffer."

Ale was still asleep. Adolfo kissed him on the cheek. As the policemen took him downstairs, a neighbor who worked for the block committee gave a triumphant smile.

64

"Who wants to go to the United States?"

Havana, 1980. At the police station, guards took Adolfo to an iron door and opened it. A stultifying heat and the stench of urine stopped his breath. It seemed completely dark.

When his eyes adjusted, he could discern three or four silhouettes moving in the shadows.

"What did you do?" someone asked in a jailbird's voice.

"My name is Adolfo Rivero Caro," he said quite firmly. "I am a lawyer,[99] and the police are making an example of me for political reasons."

The sound of his own voice gave him life again. They'd dragged him in here on a phony charge, and the reason was obvious. Knowing he intended to leave the country, they didn't want him to slip out via the embassy of Peru.

In the streets of Havana an extraordinary situation was unfolding. People were streaming into the embassy – not in tens or in hundreds but in thousands. Within the span of 72 hours, nearly eleven thousand Cubans had packed the embassy rooms and yard until not an inch of ground remained.

President Jimmy Carter, who had been working diligently to improve US-Cuban relations, decided he would tune Fidel

---

[99] A few years earlier Adolfo had completed the law degree that he had missed obtaining in the 1950's, when Havana University suspended its academic activity. See Chapter 5, "Winds of change," above.

up a bit. He announced that the United States would receive all Cubans who wished to come to American shores – an announcement quickly followed by statements from Cuban-American leaders that they would supply boats to take the refugees to Florida.

Fidel announced right back that he would permit the departure of all Cubans who wanted to leave. If Carter's move had been roughhousing, Fidel's counter was Don Corleone on a grand scale.

Having spent a week in the Havana police dungeon – the worst of his life – Adolfo had landed in Combinado del Este, the same prison his brother had left six months earlier.

Rumors, the electric energy of a prison, coursed through Combinado's tremendous interior, the current running visibly from cage to cage. Then you heard and saw for yourself. Guards were hurrying up and down the corridors, yelling: "Who wants to go to the United States? Who wants to go to the United States?" And they were pulling open the cell doors.

Such were the fruits of President Carter's policy – a mega-hurricane of humanity set loose by one leader and cordially invited by the other to storm through America's gates.[100]

Pandemonium had broken free in the massive Cuban prison. To the prisoners it made no sense. Was it a trick? What was this talk of the United States? Where would they really wind up if they allowed themselves to be taken from their cells?

The prisoners most hated by the guards were going nowhere – political prisoners who didn't even have the consolation of living with others like themselves. Because they had been picked up on charges like theft or currency fraud, they were housed with

---

[100] See the CIA's earlier, boastful statements to Emi about the Carter policy in Chapter 62, "Sophistication," above.

common criminals. All around them killers, rapists and thieves were getting an open door, while they themselves had to stay put and watch it happen.

Between spring and summer more than 120,000 of Cuba's people made an exodus from the port city of Mariel, heading to Florida in any vessel that would carry them over the water. From Combinado it was the tough guys who went – guys on death row, lifers, and others with little to lose.

The country, it seemed, had an inexhaustible supply of prisoners. Almost as soon as Combinado had emptied out, it filled right back up again. Many of the new inmates were people who had tried to leave the country illegally.

Illegally? Yes, illegally. Fidel was now throwing people in jail for doing the same thing that he had only yesterday pulled people out of jail to do.

The window of the Peru embassy and the corridor to the United States had slammed shut. America resumed its talks with the Castro regime and stopped the free entry of Cubans – while Fidel cancelled the right to emigrate as abruptly as he had given it.

Of course the human emotions aroused by Mariel would not be turned off so readily. People kept trying to get out of Cuba by boat. As often as not they were caught by Fidel's police.

When the arrested boat-people entered Combinado they were mixed in with prisoners their own age. Combinado had four populations: common prisoners under 21, common prisoners over 21, homosexuals of all ages, and political prisoners. The young boat-people were not happy to be in with young toughs. The boat-kids were ordinary youngsters who wanted to leave the country, while the prisoners their age were abnormally violent and cruel. The boat-kids asked prison authorities to move them in with older common prisoners or with political prisoners.

After trying and failing to get a response, a group of boat-kids decided to act. When they were let out into the prison yard for sun, they refused to go back to their cells until the chief of the prison came and spoke to them. Instead of the prison chief it was the garrison that showed up.

"Hey, stop! That's murder! You can't kill those kids!" Screams and shouts rippled through the cages. Adolfo jumped to the window and pushed his head into the bars.

Never had he seen such brutality.

Police were mauling the kids with sticks and clubs, flat sides of sabers, machetes and bayonets. They were even kicking and punching the kids who had fallen unconscious. The yard filled with noise of the blows and victims' screams, while hundreds of imprisoned men at their windows roared and cursed as they saw the kids being pulverized.

Guards in the buildings ran screaming through the hallways. "Who's in here for illegal exit?" One guy not far from Adolfo, who had been asleep when the riot broke loose, heard the question about illegal exit and drowsily came forward. He was seized by guards, pulled downstairs, thrown into the mêlée and beaten up.

The boat-kids were put on trial for resisting, disobeying and striking police officers. The best independent lawyers in Havana defended the kids. They produced hospital records showing heavy bruises on the guards' knuckles and toes. They tore the state's attorney to pieces.

The court found against all the boat-kids and gave them extra time of up to 15 years.

In the wake of the riot Adolfo heard intriguing snatches about human rights – a concept he considered irrelevant to Cuba. The stories were interwoven with the name of another political inmate whom Adolfo slightly knew: Ricardo Bofill.

Like Adolfo, Bofill was a lawyer and Party militant who had been caught in the microfaction trap. He had been director of publicity for Fruticuba, an official company of the time, whose directors had come up against Fidel in an almost comical way.

As everyone in Cuban politics knew, Fidel did not rule by going to an office, holding meetings or making decisions in an intelligible way. Fidel had no schedule or routine of any kind. In power he followed the habit of the outlawed fighter he had been, which was to have no habits or patterns. He had immense energy, the day was never long enough for him; he was always on his toes, moving with an entourage of armed men, carrying a loaded weapon, ready for battle. No one knew where he would eat or sleep. Every day, in each of his many homes throughout Cuba, maids turned down his bed and cooks prepared his meals in case he was coming. You never knew where to find him. At the same time you thought twice about acting without his approval because, if he happened to turn up and dislike what you had done, the consequences would be heavy. Armed not just with a pistol but with a steely conviction in himself, and with an inhumanly perfect memory that gave him the verbal tools he needed to convince almost anyone of his omniscience, he crisscrossed the country on planes, in boats, cars or jeeps, going where he saw fit, making decisions for everyone at every level of society wherever he went. In his own mind he was fully equipped not just to make political choices but to cure sickness, to design technologies, to bake bricks, run shops, teach classes, pitch baseball, or referee family disputes. Nothing that any Cuban might do was beyond his reach.

So it happened that the commander-in-chief showed up at Fruticuba to look things over and give his views.

The fruit growers had been working with citrus experts from Israel, maybe the best in the world, trying to determine optimum growing conditions for their crop. The Israelis had advised growing the fruit in numerical lots of x by y. When Fidel saw the plans for citrus production he said, "X by y is too small. You have to increase the yield and grow the fruits in lots of p by q."

Bofill and the Fruticuba directors, like Adolfo and his buddies, hadn't gotten the message about obeying the chief no matter what. So when Fidel came along and said, "Grow the fruits in lots of p by q," the Fruticuba people answered that x by y was already working pretty well.

A short time later, when Fidel's brother and second-in-command Raúl unveiled the so-called microfaction conspiracy, the Fruticuba directors were high on the honor roll.

Bofill lost his positions in society and watched his life crumble. Unlike Adolfo he also went to jail, where he sustained the hardest blows of all. His parents died without his being able to tell them goodbye; and he succumbed to rehabilitation.

Misfortune turned him into a desperate man. After his release he got on public buses in Havana and said aloud to no one in particular: "The Castro brothers are gangsters. Do you know the country is being run by a pair of gangsters?"

People shifted toward the other end of the bus, thinking he was a crazy man – which he was – and expecting police to board at any moment, which somehow they didn't.

Now Security had arrested Bofill to keep him from running to the embassy of Peru. Fidel and his circle, while ignoring the rest of the populace, had been obsessed by the thought of a few hundred purged ex-officials who might seize the opportunity to slip out of Cuba.

Everyone, it seemed, had a skeleton or two. Adolfo's was «Zarathustra», the 80-page document that police had taken from his apartment.[101] As he was brought to interrogation and the rigmarole began, it seemed his fears were on target.

"Certain papers were found in your home," they said.

---

[101] See Chapters 54 & 63, above.

True, he said, he had some leaflets.

"Those are not leaflets. They are drafts and sketches for propaganda papers. You were helping Bofill prepare those papers, weren't you?"

Nothing of the kind, he answered; they were just odd leaflets.

"How did they come into your possession?"

He couldn't say. Lots of people had given him papers over the years.

"What else can you tell you tell us about Bofill?"

That was the key. They didn't want him at all. They wanted Bofill.

"I hardly know Bofill!" Adolfo said cleanly and buoyantly. Seeing they had nowhere to go with him, they ended the exchange.

Adolfo, however, had gotten quite a nugget from them. Bofill's unknown human-rights campaign had become a serious concern to the state. Now that was an opportunity.

65

In the Parthenon

Combinado del Este, 1980-82. Adolfo started to visit Bofill in the other man's prison quarters. Bofill happened to live in a cell, more private than a *galera*. His fellow activists Elizardo Sánchez and Enrique Hernández also lived close by, so Bofill's was an ideal meeting place.

"Tell me about your group," Adolfo asked Bofill. "You say you have everything organized. What's your program, your ideology, your strategy?"

"We have none of that. Everything is above board. Nothing is hidden. We don't conspire."

"But that's fatal. How do you manage without those things?"

"The question is, how would I manage with *those* things. Fidel has defeated every program, ideology, strategy and conspiracy that goes against him. The way to beat him is to stand up and refuse to take shit while giving him nothing to attack."

"And how do you do that?"

"Look, this government can do anything it wants. You know it and I know it. But the government can't say it does anything it wants. It has to *pretend* people have some rights. They have to obey the constitution. I know, the constitution is crap. Everybody knows it's crap. But the constitution is important because it gives you a space in which to work. It's a tiny space – a tiny, tiny space, a *minimum* space – but you can work in it.

"So when the government is screwing over some guys we just tell the government: Look, you can't screw over those guys, the law doesn't allow you. And guess what. It's true! They can't tell you to shut up because that would be forbidding you to speak. The government never admits to taking away your right to speak. The most they ever do is *intimidate* you from using your right. They can't accuse you of ideological deviation because you're using the law, which is *their* fucking ideology!

"Okay, they can throw you in jail but sooner or later they have to let you out. Their best tactic is to ignore you. If your boss ignores you, you write a letter to *his* boss. Pretty soon you are writing to the national bosses, then to the bosses of international communism. Finally, when nothing else works, you write to the international human-rights organizations. You are making all this noise – and Fidel doesn't have a goddamn fucking thing to say about it!"

Adolfo: "You mean that's all there is to it? Telling them they can't screw over so-and-so? That's the big idea they're so scared of?"

"That's it."

"But you've got to have a program! How else do you expect to win people to your ideas?"

"The basic idea is not to take shit from sons of whores. It might not sound like a big idea but actually it is. Everyone has it deep inside. So we're going to demonstrate it and hold open the door for other people to join."

"How many are you?"

"Let's see – Elizardo, Enrique, myself – right now it's the three of us."

"You are *three?* That's what you mean by having things organized?"

"How many people did Fidel have when he started out in the

Sierra? Twenty? Ten? Five?"

"On that point you are absolutely correct," Adolfo said.

"The point is not how many you have but how many you *might* have. It begins from one. From one you get three or four. Three or four people who put their minds to it can change a country."

"And what about your strategy?"

"Our strategy is to have no strategy. That way no one can figure out our next move. Many times even I don't know what I'm going to do before I do it. Of course that means Security doesn't know either, and they can't use their methods on me."

How curious, Adolfo thought dismissively – but then, as he reflected on the beating of the boat-kids, Bofill's idea took hold of him.

Adolfo became a regular visitor to Bofill's cell. For the first time in years he had a new excitement for what he loved best. Instead of wearing widow's black for the socialist idea, Adolfo could take the part of actual people whom the system had mistreated.

Bofill, with lines of information everywhere, had bags of stories about guys who had been beaten up. For Adolfo those stories were the limit. Even after his personal downfall he had insisted in letters to his parents: *Yes, people go to prison here because they have acted against the state, but the authorities mistreat no one, beatings are unheard-of.*

And now, every day, Bofill had stories of new beatings.

As Adolfo recalled the many bulletins or 'bullets' of his that had gone out of Combinado, his thoughts ineluctably returned to the evening some other prisoners approached him with a funny request.

"Hey, lawyer! Later on we're doing a play trial on the second floor.

Four other lawyers are coming. You come too! It's going to be really interesting!"

"I don't think so," Adolfo said, annoyed. "Jumping from floor to floor isn't easy. Anyway, you already have four lawyers. What do you want with me?"

"Look teacher, the men asked for you by name."

"If you insist, I'll come. But send someone to fetch me."

At the appointed hour a small, bespectacled man entered Adolfo's *galera*. Everyone called him J.J. He was a physicist who had murdered his wife. J.J. was on patrol duty with his partner, a man with Asiatic features.

"Where's the lawyer?" J.J. called out.

"Right here, J.J."

"Come with us," J.J. said. "I have to talk to you."

The three of them went out of the *galera*.

"Listen J.J., I don't feel like going. You've already got four lawyers."

J.J. grinned. "Yeah, but the other four have just been released from the prison."

"All right, goddamit, I'll go!"

J.J. paused and looked incredulously at Adolfo. "You haven't caught on, have you."

"Caught on to what?"

"Your release just came in."

Adolfo was stunned. "You're joking."

"Nobody jokes about that. It came a few minutes ago. The other releases have already left. Now get yourself together and beat it."

They shook hands. Other men came up to Adolfo. "Brother, I'll miss you!" "Teacher, say hello to the streets for us!"

He went back to the *galera* in a state of shock.

The *galera* had emptied out, the men off in the TV room. Adolfo went to his bunk and slowly packed his bag.

Men trickled in. They'd heard about his release and wanted to say goodbye. They hugged him, teased him, took stuff away from him.

Before he knew it, he was outside the building.

An officer was waiting to take him into another building. Someone handed him an envelope with his personal documents. A patrolman took him into yet another building and into a room with enormous shelves, thousands of packages. The patrolman read a card, pulled a package off a shelf and gave it to Adolfo.

"These are your clothes."

Adolfo opened the package and found the clothes he was wearing when he'd been arrested nearly two years before. He took the bundle off to the side and donned each article one by one.

The patrolman showed him to a door and pointed outside. "Follow that road. It goes to the highway. You'll find a bus stop there."

"I haven't got any money," Adolfo was self-possessed enough to say.

"You'll be okay. The drivers know."

As he walked away from two years of his life, the thought occurred that they were chucking him out of prison exactly the way they'd chucked him in.

Midnight had gone when Adolfo alighted at the bus stop near his house. He looked up to his place. Lights were still on. He took a quick glance around and started up the stairs, his clothes now feeling very crumpled.

The apartment door was open, someone at the entrance talking to Marisa: Carlos Menéndez, an Afro-Cuban economist and, it seemed, Marisa's lover. Adolfo had known the other man since his student days and liked him. Carlos, hearing footsteps, looked down and saw Adolfo.

"We have a visit," he told Marisa.

The men embraced. Adolfo went in, looked around and gave Marisa a peck on the cheek. She had tears in her eyes and was working to keep control.

"We've been waiting for you," she said. "Your case came to trial. You were found guilty and sentenced to a year. Since you'd already served nearly two, the judge ordered you released immediately. That was three days ago." She paused. "I'll wake Alejandro."

"How do you feel?" Carlos asked.

"Stunned. This is a complete surprise to me."

Ale appeared in his pajamas. He ran to his papi and gave him a huge hug.

"Were you expecting me?" Adolfo said.

"Always!" the boy said jubilantly.

Carlos said goodbye. Marisa took Ale back to bed while Adolfo made for his library. He had a long look at the room, drinking it in until his energy quit. A youngster camping out on a starlit evening in the Parthenon would not have been more dazzled than Adolfo was, going to sleep on his library sofa that night.

66

Forever young

{Emi Rivero's recollections}

Miami, 1983. "I remember how I held you in my arms, cradling and putting you to sleep. You smiled at me, held out your arms and touched my teeth. My teeth caught your attention."

It has been said that some people gain an aura, a light, a purification of sorts when death comes near. My mother was always a person of very strong will, extremely feminine, loving to her whole family, but with a tough core that we all knew quite well. With us, her kids, she was a disciplinarian. But in her last two years, when she felt the beyond at her fingertips, her nature changed noticeably.

She poured out her memories of marriage, of my early youth; of how big my head was and how everyone teased her about it; of how poor we were; of her sewing diapers from political banners; of our trips to the country; of my great-uncle José Manuel and his game-cocks; of Adolfito's birth, how beautiful he was and how easy it was to love him. I encouraged her to reminisce because, when she did, my mother became young again.

Not a single time when we were together, or when I spoke with her by phone, did she fail to mention my brother. "Remember Adolfito. Get Adolfito out of Cuba." It became her obsession.

Our mother had been a fearless protector of both her sons. A few years earlier, when she was working as an elevator operator at one of the Miami Beach hotels, Henry Kissinger stepped into her cab. As she delivered the famous statesman to his floor, she didn't miss a chance to tell him about her two sons who were political detainees in Cuba. And of course, being Kissinger, he took a note about it.[102]

Failing health did not keep *la vieja* from working for Adolfito's release. She wrote to Gabriel García Márquez, asking the writer to intervene with Fidel. García Márquez had an extremely strong tie to Fidel and at times rescued Fidel from his own craziness by obtaining freedom for people whom Fidel would otherwise have destroyed.

García Márquez wrote back to my mother, telling her: Madame, I did what you asked and believe me, it was not easy. When Adolfito was let out of Combinado at the beginning of 1982, it seemed that my mother and García Márquez might have had something to do with it.

In 1983 *la vieja* was dying of laryngeal cancer. Adolfito was on the street in Havana, fighting openly against Castro. I visited our mother in the hospital during a difficult surgery; a portion of her nose had been replaced with a flap that the surgeons had grafted. Even coming out of anesthesia, she gave all her energy to tell me I should enter Cuba clandestinely and bring Adolfito to the US.

La vieja died in Miami in September 1983 at the age of 72. She had been the center of her family, and her death fell hard on everyone. When her elder brother Ramón, who had stayed in Cuba, got the news, he lay down on his bed and did not get up again.

---

[102] In 2014 Kissinger, in his tenth decade, was taken severely to task by Western media over the revelation that he and President Ford, some 38 years earlier, had considered attacking Cuba for its armed intervention in Angola. In telling this story, journalists fell into the trap of historical narration 21st-century style; they forgot all about the Cold War. So their accounts failed to note that Fidel, in sending troops to Angola, had acted as a Soviet surrogate. https://www. nytimes.com/2014/10/01/world/americas/kissinger-drew-up-plans-to-attack-cuba-records-show.html?searchResultPosition=1

67

A chorus line

1982-87. After Adolfo's release from prison, Security heard or saw nearly everything he did: every call he made, every book or parcel he brought, every visit he received. Adolfo made friends with the guys who were tailing him.

Bofill did not stop confronting the regime. His house was a stash of leaflets, documents, foreign books and magazines – a political firetrap of the most blatant kind.

Police and Defense Committee members came to harass him at all hours. Typically they met his wife Yolanda Miyares, a beautiful *mulata* who, when driven to anger, was terrifying. People coming to annoy Ricardo made her angry. Yola defended her husband with courage and ferocity, scaring the intruders away.

Police nabbed Bofill on one charge after another. He went in and out of Combinado with such frequency that the big prison became a second home to him – or perhaps a first home.

Whenever Bofill sojourned at Combinado he sent human-rights bulletins or 'bullets' to Adolfo. They were tales of abuse, carried from the prison by visitors who used an array of ingenious means to smuggle them past the guards.

Those bullets were the only things Adolfo concealed from the Security men. Nor did he share them with Marisa, who as a loyal cadre of the regime would certainly have disapproved.

In solitary labor Adolfo recast those stories for transmission to the wider world.

The United States government had started making radio broadcasts to Cuba, just as it had been doing for decades to the Soviet Bloc nations. The broadcasts of Radio Martí, named for Cuba's patriarch, were winning big audiences on the island. Somehow the station was getting human-rights stories from Combinado. The airwaves in Cuba filled up with them.

Security tightened the screws on the group of activists. As Adolfo thought about an illegal exit, Bofill – now out of Combinado – took an action of his own: he entered the French embassy and asked for asylum.

With that action Bofill meant to do several things at a stroke: raise a public fuss about the human-rights situation in Cuba; create diplomatic problems for Fidel; and find a way out of the country for himself and his group.

The French admitted Bofill, even as they saw the bind in which he was putting them.

At once the Cuban government protested, demanding Bofill's removal from the embassy.

It was exactly the faceoff Bofill had wanted. But then the French took another step. They confined him to a room with a guard, allowing him no outside contacts – no visits, no phone calls, nothing.

It was actually worse than prison. From Combinado Bofill had waged a war of words. From the French embassy he couldn't pass a syllable.

On top of that, he had left his cohorts exposed. Within hours Adolfo, Elizardo and Enrique had been seized and locked up in Security.

Radio Martí jumped on the moving train, broadcasting continuous bulletins: Human-rights activist Ricardo Bofill a prisoner in France's Havana embassy! The directors of Cuba's human-rights committee arrested by State Security!

Interrogations were much more urgent this time. Adolfo's questioners had turned into a chorus-line of Salomés, dancing for John the Baptist's head.

Rivero Caro, they told him, *you will croak in this place unless you give us all the worms.* Fidel's gracious old term, *gusanos,*[103] had been brought out of storage to slime Bofill's colleagues and helpers in the human-rights campaign.

From Adolfo Security wanted two things. First of all they wanted Bofill. Then they wanted the 'Ho Chi Minh trail' – or so Adolfo called the network of exit-paths by which the human-rights messages left the country.[104]

Bofill was sitting safe in an embassy, so no need to worry about him. The Ho Chi Minh trail was not secure, it had spurs and exposures all over Havana, and that was a problem.

Adolfo's part of the relay began when he got a call from the mother of one of Bofill's runners. "Adolfo, why not stop by tonight, I am cooking up something nice for dinner." The main course was a bullet that the runner had taken from Combinado.

At times Adolfo got two or more calls on the same bullet – Bofill sending the message by multiple runners to make sure of getting it through. Each time Adolfo typed up the message in the form of a letter and made the next move on the trail.

---

[103] *Gusanos,* literally "worms," is a term that the revolutionary regime applied to its Cuban opponents, especially to those who fled to the US. Fidel himself had put the term away during his negotiations with Jimmy Carter. But he and his supporters gladly reprised it for use against the human-rights activists. Some epithets never die, and *gusano* seems to be one of them. As of this writing, Fidel's fans in the US continue to use the term for opponents of Cuba's regime.
[104] The system of routes by which North Vietnam supplied its forces fighting against foreign armies in South Vietnam; see https://en.wikipedia.org/wiki/Ho_Chi_Minh_trail

{in the garden of Maxim, an ambassador from Europe}

Maxim: Look at my plants! Aren't they splendid? What a climate for growing – and only fifty dollars in fertilizer!

Adolfo: Friend, for fifty dollars you could have bought the whole Botanical Garden.

Maxim: I don't care about the Botanical Garden. I care about my garden!

Adolfo: Listen, I heard from Bofill. He's in the monastery.

Maxim (looking away): Ah yes, the eastern monastery – but not in India.[105]

Adolfo: The thing is, I have another letter. Would you mind sending it to the North?

Maxim: Let's see – a letter from the East going South to North – a North which happens to be in the West. The Lord loves a compass!

Someone else carried the letter to Maxim. He dropped it in the diplomatic pouch for his capital city. There it entered the postal system and gained a speedy, secure passage to Adolfo's recipient – most often to Emi's brother in Washington DC.

Not long afterward a story appeared in some foreign medium about the mistreatment of prisoners in Cuban jails. In every case Radio Martí broadcast the item to a mass audience in Cuba.

Castro and his henchmen went berserk over those broadcasts. The police, who were experts in the higher math of intrigue, surely knew how the human-rights stories were getting out. Their inability to stop them only multiplied their fury.

---

[105] Combinado del Este, the "Eastern complex"

Now at last, with Adolfo in interrogation, they had their enemy under their thumbs. They couldn't charge Maxim because he was a diplomat; but they could use him against Adolfo and did it with relish.

"How did the letters go out? Was it through your friend Maxim?"

Maxim is leaving the country in two or three months. If I name him, Security will go to his bosses and tell them: You have to get rid of Maxim. His bosses will agree without even changing his departure date. Anyway, those bosses are not so fond of Fidel right now. They will think better of Maxim because he helped us.

Okay, no harm if I give them Maxim.

"As a matter of fact it was through Maxim," Adolfo candidly told his interrogators.

Having gotten Maxim, Adolfo's interrogators went for the Ho Chi Minh trail.

"Lots of people were involved," Adolfo said. "Each time they were different. They used to call me up and say, 'Come and eat with us.' I don't remember exactly who they were."

"You expect us to believe that?"

"What can I say? It's the truth," he answered with one of those little-boy shrugs that can conquer anyone.

They bore down on him quite intently. Adolfo noticed another man at the back of the room working a video camera.

"It's a very bad thing for you that you have been working with this son of a whore Bofill," the interrogators told him.

Adolfo stayed quiet.

"You are a man with certain privileges in this society."

Really! Tell me about them.

"This is a workers' society. And you live without working. That's a privilege."

Oh, yeah? You should try it.   •

"Your son also has privileges. He attends a higher school for mathematics, true? And if he stays there he can have quite a good career."

It had been one of the sweetest episodes of his parenthood. When Ale was ready for high school he applied to a superior school that had hundreds of applicants and 14 openings. The boy was so smart that no one doubted he would get in.

But then Marisa started to worry he might not make it. She and Adolfo went spiraling down until Víctor – a family friend and alumnus of 'the monastery' – paid a visit.

Víctor put death into his eyes and screamed at the pair of them. "How dare you talk like that? Fourteen openings! If they had just one opening you would have no right to doubt he will make it!"

Ale got in – and now Adolfo had to hear about it from these hoodlums.

They want me to denounce Bofill. They are going to make my life damned unpleasant until I do it – and not just my life either.

Let's reason it out. Where am I and where is Bofill? I am in a dungeon. Bofill is in the French embassy. What would Bofill do if he were here? He would give the denunciation. It isn't worth a shit, and if they try to use it later I can just take it back.

Okay, I'm going to denounce Bofill.

"Ricardo Bofill has turned his back on Cuba! Ricardo Bofill has betrayed the revolution! Ricardo Bofill is a traitor to socialism!"

It was a full denunciation, spectacular in its breadth and vehemence. Adolfo's interrogators got it all on camera; they were so full of glee they couldn't contain themselves.

Once back in his cell he lay down on the bunk bed and wondered: Where the hell is Adri?

68

Best foot forward

1987. Adolfo's most regular visitor in Security was his cousin Sonia, a family angel who had seen Emi through his decades in jail. Every week Sonia brought Adolfo his news. The day she told him that Adriana had called her was one of the happiest Adolfo could remember. "The pigeon appeared! The pigeon appeared!" he said to everyone.

In Sonia's next visits Adolfo heard nothing more from the pigeon. But that was Adri; her comings and goings were not to be understood.

Adri's mother, Rita R., was an independent journalist and fellow traveler in the Bofill campaign. She wanted her 14-year-old daughter to learn English. Bofill had told her about Adolfo, an expert English-language tutor.

On the appointed day Adri, not wanting to be late to her first lesson, came to Adolfo's building an hour ahead and sat on the stairs inside. Afterward Adolfo went to his terrace to read and watch for the arriving student. All approaches were visible from the terrace.

As he had not seen her coming, Adolfo was amazed to hear her knock at the door. He asked her: "What are you, spirit matter? Did you materialize from thin air?"

Adri answered as she answered most anything. She laughed.

Adri had a tremendous aptitude. She also tired quickly. If she didn't get something at a stroke, she pushed it away. So went the English language. "*¡Coño!* Why should I speak that stuff anyway!" she said, laughing.

Anyone else Adolfo would have shown the door. Adri got her way. He laughed along with her – a notable development for a man who had gone through life with a sardonic smile.

Adolfo was a bookworm, so attached to his reading that only an important political matter or the force of love for his son could pull him away from it. Then that slip of a girl told him: "Look, put your book down and come with me!" To his surprise he obeyed, laughing.

From her mother Adri knew the language of Bofill's campaign, and she did not feel shy about challenging Adolfo's viewpoints. Adolfo loved the audacity of it. He found that Adri had keen insights, especially about young people's reactions to an idea or a possible action. Bofill, whom Adri addressed as an equal, called her his friend.

Adri fell hard for Adolfo; they became lovers. With Adri he played as never before. He was happy without knowing it – the purest happiness possible.

Now he sat in Security, waiting on her call. Where was she? Weeks had gone by since that last message. Sonia hadn't heard a thing from her or from Víctor either.

Adolfo couldn't understand. After much labor he told himself: *Don't burn your brains out. Life is not a syllogism. You can't always interpret it. Whatever the reason is, you'll find out later.*

He saw the walls of his apartment. Grey matter had spread itself through the rooms; grey books, grey windows, grey picture-frames blocking landscapes in grey, a beautiful woman with grey hair.

Víctor appeared in a brilliant white suit and hugged him. Adolfo went out into the street, gliding across a city on crutches. Up came the street that led to Adri's house. Adri was running to him; dressed in black and white, her lips bright red, pursing with joy.

Adolfo threw his arm around her. They went jauntily along and Adriana said: Tell me about it! She was asking about his release.

He looked and looked and saw nothing. Adri, he said, this is a dream. No! she insisted. This isn't a dream, this is real! He said: Adri, I'm telling you, it's a dream. He stopped and backed away from her. Back, back and poof! He woke up.

Adolfo's cousin Sonia came for a visit and told him: "Marisa called with some news. Your friend Ricardo went to see her but she wouldn't receive him in the house."

Adolfo jumped. Bofill was in the street! Not in the embassy, not in Security, not behind someone else's walls. How?

They must have worked out a deal. Bofill would go out of the embassy, and in return Security would not arrest him. Okay. What about Adolfo and the other guys in Security? Bofill would never take a deal that left them out – never.

Days went by with no more news. After lunch Adolfo listened to his cellmate sleeping.

Voices came from the corridor. Unusual; guards did not talk to each other in the hall. Must be a guard speaking through an open cell door, giving instructions to a prisoner. Footsteps, a door clanging shut – his door opened.

"Rivero Caro. Follow!"

An interrogation? No, they were leading him another way. It went on and on. What the hell! He felt his insides go liquid; his heart was ticking like a bomb.

"Permission to enter!" his escort said in a loud voice. "Forward!" came the answer. He was led into a large office. Two colonels from the Ministry were waiting.

"Hey! What's the matter? Don't you recognize me?" one of them said like an old friend.

Adolfo stayed quiet.

"I am Blanco. I am the interrogator of your brother! I came to see you at the Socialist Youth. I have remembered you guys for 25 years. You were great, both of you!"

That was an interesting choice of words.

All those years ago this colonel, as a State Security interrogator, had come to get help from Adolfo, a high official in the Communist Party. Adolfo's brother had been caught plotting against Fidel; Blanco was the man in charge of the case. The prisoner was a handful, and Blanco had sought Adolfo's help.

In the intervening years Adolfo had scarcely thought about the interview – but now he did not wonder that the other man should recall him.

"I've just got one thing to ask you," Blanco said. "When is this shit going to stop?" He meant the human-rights protests.

What are you asking me for? I'm the one in jail, Adolfo thought.

Blanco explained. "I know you. I can't see what you are doing with sons of whores like Bofill and Sánchez. They aren't worthy of you."

Adolfo gave the shrug he had practiced to perfection: *How should I know? I'm a good fellow!*

"Listen," Blanco said. "This government is not going to fall."

How about that! He's concerned about the government falling.

"I've just become director of this installation. We're in the middle of changing things around."

Adolfo smiled.

"Okay, that's all for now," Blanco concluded. "It's good seeing you again."

Jesus! Adolfo thought. *The sky is still up there and I'm still down here.* His walk back to the cell was a lot shorter.

In two days he was out.

"Unbelievable! Unbelievable! The whole thing has changed!" Bofill was ecstatic. "Fidel had to give in because it was raining shit! Everything worked. Radio Martí really worked. We're famous! People are talking about us all over the country! That's why they had to put a stop to the thing and let us out. They promised not to re-arrest any of us but of course I didn't believe them. I went straight home from the embassy, I had a shave and a shower and waited for the Security van to come. All kinds of people were showing up, just to meet me and thank me for what we're doing. I thought, this can't be for real! One guy said, I'm a farmer from Pinar del Río,[106] I heard about your campaign on the radio and I just want to tell you it's fantastic, I'm behind you a hundred percent. All I could say was: Come on in and we'll have a coffee. Unbelievable!"

"Look," Adolfo said grimly, "I have to tell you something."

"What?"

"I denounced you."

"Forget it! In your place I'd have done the same thing."

"That's not all. They have it on camera."

"Don't worry! We'll call *Efe*,[107] we'll say they forced a denunciation from you in Security, and if the sons of whores try to use it against us it's worthless."

---

[106] Cuba's westernmost province, hours away from Havana
[107] Major Spanish news agency

"Okay! Great!" Adolfo said – then, to himself: *That's too easy. He's got to feel it in some way.*

"Marisa is furious," Víctor told him when they met. "After they picked you up, she told me to stay away from Ale. I didn't listen to her. I kept talking to Ale, giving him news, keeping him up with developments. Marisa found out and hit the roof."

"You did exactly the right thing."

"Of course! And besides, I didn't go near your cousin Sonia. When I found out Adri had called her, I told her not to do it again."

"What for? I trust Sonia one hundred percent!"

"She might have talked to Marisa. It was just a feeling." Víctor looked at Adolfo with his eyes of a faithful hunting-dog.

"Forget it, buddy. Everything's fine now."

When he met Adri she swung her arms around him, crying out for joy – and he felt as high and rowdy as a helium balloon.

The nucleus of human-rights activists in Havana had grown to include dozens of people. On a Sunday they met at a church in the still-handsome old part of the city.

As people were talking in small groups on the sidewalk a black van appeared, moving along in front of them at microscopic speed. Everybody knew it was a Security van filming them.

A natty young fellow stepped forward, produced a comb from his pocket and began to fix his hair. "Hey! If they're going to take pictures of me I want to look my best!"

Adolfo faced the van and took out a comb. So did the other men. They stared straight at the van, a line of men combing their hair.

69

Addio Casablanca

Havana, March 1988. Adolfo climbed up on a table
and announced: "Ladies and gentlemen! Welcome to this
exhibition! We are featuring painters and artists from the Cuban
counterculture. In other countries the establishment plays cricket
with the counterculture. Here the big shots play a rougher game
and we have to be on our toes."

The owners of a handsome house in the middle of the city had
moved almost all their furniture out of it to make room for
an impromptu art gallery. Dozens of people were enjoying the
exhibit.

An elegant-looking American couple admired a painting by
Adolfo's friend Nicolás Guillén Landrián. "What do all those little
phantoms mean?" the gentleman said to Nicolás. "Such keen eyes!
What are they looking for?"

"They are spermatozoids within the man's sexual organ, and they
are looking for a woman to assault," Nicolás said plainly.

The American lady was dumbstruck. Adolfo swallowed his
laughter.

Foreign reporters were talking to Cubans who complained about
the behavior of State Security officers. A man with a notepad
approached Adolfo – clearly a Security agent.

"You know," Adolfo told him, "the food in Security is not bad."

As night fell and people were leaving the house in clusters, Adolfo
got back up on the table and announced: "Next Saturday we'll

meet here again! This is going to remain a permanent exhibition – a human-rights club in the heart of Havana."

Bofill was jubilant. "No one has ever done this to the Castro regime – no one!"

"It's been fantastic! Unbelievable!" Adriana exclaimed.

Next Saturday the group was much smaller and somehow grimmer. Three or four unhappy women had come to tell reporters about their experiences with Security.

Bofill announced to reporters: "I've just called to a few embassies and they all tell me the same thing. Someone called up and said the meeting was not going to take place. Obviously it's Security. Please, before you talk with us, talk with these women. They are the ones that Castro and the government must face!"

People were knocking hard at the door. The owner René, an ex-bodybuilder, opened and found a cluster of a dozen people.

"I am the president of the Committee for the Defense of the Revolution!" one man proclaimed. "We know that a counterrevolutionary meeting is going on in this house and we are not going to put up with it!"

"We have nothing secret or underground here," René answered. "This is an open activity that is going on in *my house*."

"We are not going to put up with it!" the man repeated.

Others were shouting. "*¡Gusanos!* Counterrevolutionaries! Go to the US! Down with the worms!"

The protesters made a move to enter the house. The sight of René's impressive bulk gave them pause. But the unfriendly crowd was growing. By now 40 or 50 people had gathered.

A few of the Defense Committee people pushed in. René was

about to assault them when Bofill intervened. "No, René! No violence! The only violence is theirs!"

The crowd poured into the house. Security people took photos and looked for incriminating details. The counter-counterrevolution was getting rowdy.

Bofill yelled to Adolfo. "Go and make some phone calls! We'll settle things here."

Adolfo bounded away from the rear of the house at the same time Adriana was coming up to the front. Seeing the crowd, she tightened her fists and screamed: "Let me pass! Let me pass! I want to see their faces!"

People took her for a righteous revolutionary full of class hatred. The diminutive 16-year-old was giving a first-rate performance. The crowds parted, letting her approach the door.

"Bofill!" she screamed. He opened the door and she jumped in. "Where's Adolfo?"

"He just left; Enrique too. We've got to call the embassies and see what can be done."

"This is fun – *real* fun!" Adri cried out and started to dance.

Nicolás the painter said: "Adolfo's little girl is crazy! She wants to fly like a bird. Hey, little girl! Are you a woman or a bird?"

The counter-counterrevolutionaries outside had swelled to a crowd in the hundreds. The air felt combustible.

The Minister of the Interior arrived. Two more ministers and a number of colonels joined him. They talked with Bofill and agreed on a peaceful breakup of the meeting. Bofill speaking with Fidel's ministers was quite a sight.

A few days later Adolfo was at home arranging flowers when he heard a knock at the door. He opened and found one of the

Security officers assigned to watch him – a man with whom Adolfo had grown almost friendly.

"Hey!" the Security man said. "I told you it was going to get serious. Didn't I tell you?"

"Yeah," Adolfo answered, "you told me."

"Okay, now it's serious."

The phone rang. It was Bofill. "We have to meet. Pick up Enrique and come over."

Adolfo took off right away without trying to lose the Security man – everything above board, nothing covert.

On his way to Enrique's he grabbed the morning paper and turned to the editorials. Almost before he registered the details, his intestines filled up with an old, familiar feeling.

It was a huge editorial, covering half a page. *Human rights gangster group – Revolution stabbed in the back – Counterrevolutionaries' attack at UN meeting in Geneva.*

The piece was extremely rough in tone and earnest at the same time. Adolfo thought: *Not even my fucking mother would speak to me after reading this.*

He put down the paper and stormed into Enrique's. The other man was having a quiet breakfast.

"We are in the fucking editorial of *Granma*!" Adolfo exclaimed.

Enrique looked it over coolly. "You are the one being discussed in here," he told Adolfo.

"Fidel wrote the thing himself," Adolfo said. "It's his style, I'm sure of it."

In the streets of Havana things were considerably tougher.

Concurrent with the *Granma* editorial, Cuban TV was running
a program about the human-rights movement called *La historia
de un fullero*, 'The Story of a Lying Cheat.' That last epithet was
Fidel's description of choice for Bofill.

{Adolfo's recollections}

When Bofill and I were in the street, people shouted: "That's
Bofill!" Usually they were admirers but someone could always
throw a brick. We were never afraid of people; we were only
concerned about bricks.

My friend Víctor was now working as a chess trainer to Maxim
the ambassador, a job I had gotten him. Maxim told Víctor: "I
have a friend I want you to meet."

It turned out to be a Soviet official. The Russian told Víctor: "I
know you have relations with certain people and I want you to
know we look on them with approval. Of course, if you publish
this I'll say it's a goddamn lie."

When Víctor gave me the story he said: "Look, I want you to
know about this but I don't think it's a good idea for Bofill to get
all the details. He's very emotional. On an impulse he might make
an announcement. The Russians would have to deny it and we
would have a mess."

I agreed. When I talked to Bofill I just told him we should
take more of an interest in the Soviet Union because political
conditions were right. I suggested we write a letter to Gorbachov.

Bofill went for it. "Great, fantastic, do a letter to Gorbachov."

I wrote a letter and took it to the Soviet embassy. The letter
basically said that Fidel was giving socialism a bad name and
that we were appealing to the good offices of our Soviet friends
on behalf of human rights in Cuba. The letter also said that if at
times we in the human-rights group had called on the Western
powers and not on the Soviets, it wasn't because we doubted the
Soviets' good will. It was simply that we didn't want to put them

on the spot, as we were sure they would understand.

I was as proud of this letter as of anything I've ever done.

Then all of a sudden I had my exit visa. Adri got hers as well, and the visas were for Paris.[108]

I was leaving for the airport in a matter of hours and I still had to explain to Bofill about the Soviet thing. My close friends had come to the house to be with me, and they stood in the hall talking to each other while I was at my typewriter.

Those last visits were very charged. Anyone who came was aware that Security was watching the place. In that kind of atmosphere you develop the skin of a rhinoceros. When friends decide for their own safety that they have to turn away, you understand.[109]

But the day I left, all the big ones were there. Félix came, Ezequiel came, others came, even knowing they would be on video. It was really thrilling.

Of course the toughest thing was Alejandro. I was the one who had to keep a straight face. He saw me about to break down and put his hand on my mouth. When I left the house I didn't even turn around. I knew he would be looking from the terrace. I just put up my hand to say goodbye.[110]

---

[108] Kiko Arocha writes of an accidental meeting on the street with Adolfo, who told him "with great joy that he was about to leave the country at the request of François Mitterand, president of France." Adolfo had received an offer of sponsorship from *France terre d'asile*, a nonprofit that since 1971 has supported worthy candidates for asylum.

[109] Adolfo had done it just that way with César; see Chapter 58, "Laurel & Hardy," above.

[110] Bofill departed Cuba shortly afterward. In late November 1988 he was received in the Oval Office by President Reagan, who had warm words for the human-rights campaign as well as for Bofill himself. See https://www.youtube.com/watch?v=XCjTiA6Nd8o (from 11:16).

70

The sealed train

{Emi Rivero}

Paris, May 1988. [111] Adolfito and I had been reminiscing for several days, organizing our thoughts, writing them down, trying to convey our experiences. Ours had been a divided family; one brother pitted against the other, to our parents' despair, in a merciless conflict. It was our hope that one day the Cuban people could reunite as we had.

{the two, conversing}

"If I had come to take you out of Cuba, as I had been planning to, I would have taken you and Alejandro," Emi said. "My idea was to get into Havana, call you from a public phone and just say to you like any friend: Listen, why don't you bring Alejandro and we three will go to the movies? In a couple of hours you would both have been leaving on a ship."

Adolfo: "And you would have done absolutely right! The problem was Alejandro's mother. It would have ruined her because her life is still in Cuba. She would have become a counterrevolutionary, losing her son to the drug-infested capitalist world. People would have put tremendous heat on her and the thing would have pursued her forever.

"It's part of a larger problem," Adolfo kept on, quite agitated.

---

[111] An account of this meeting appears in Adolfo Rivero Caro & Emilio Adolfo Rivero Caro, *Las cabañitas/The Little Cabins*, Miami: Alexandria Library, 2012 (twin Spanish and English volumes).

"How do you raise a kid in a socialist society – a society based on erroneous principles? Do you tell the kid the system is bad, or do you tell him to do his best? In a bad system, do you want your kid to succeed or fail?"

Adolfo paused and resumed. "It's no joke. In Alejandro's case it was a better solution not to wrench him away from his mother. At times the only solutions are the imperfect ones."

Emi: "That last comment of yours doesn't sound like my Marxist brother."

"Quite the contrary! In spite of all the evil Marxism has spread – a notion I freely concede – the Marxist viewpoint is still the best means of looking at society; far better than the misleading ideas that you and the old man had."

"Misleading?!"

"Yes, misleading. You didn't have a social perspective. You had sentimentalism."

"Better to believe in something and be destroyed for your beliefs than to believe in nothing at all."

"There, you see? Sentimental!" Adolfo exclaimed. Then, more quietly: "*Los viejos* would be happy to see us like this."

"How do you mean?"

"I'm thinking of all those phone calls they made to me when you were in prison. How I hated those calls, having to hear the old man's grief and not being able to help."

Emi: "*La vieja* said something very hard before she died. She said, 'With all the education the two of you had, you never distinguished yourselves.'"

"She was right," Adolfo said. "We never reached the old man's level. What did I do with my life? I sacrificed human values to abstractions. That should never be done. Since that time I have had my ass kicked around quite a bit, and it seems only fair."

"You never betrayed anyone," Emi said protectively. "You never turned anyone in."

Adolfo ignored that and kept on. "Probably I will get the punishment the Buddhists mention. After I die I will have to come back here and go through more lives and get my ass kicked again! But I'm not complaining. It's been a useful life."

"You know, Adolfito, I think I have been tremendously lucky in life."

"Lucky? *You?*" Adolfo was all but laughing.

"I've experienced almost everything a man can experience. When I look at people I see through their masks. It's a luxury. Life is still full of noise, but I hear the music underneath."

"It's a shame you came back to Cuba," Adolfo said sadly. "You should have known the CIA was using you. Or that the whole enterprise was doomed anyway."

"I actually had a pretty good idea both things were true."

"And you came anyway."

"I did."

"Then you didn't have the courage of your convictions! You should have stayed in the States and waited for the right moment."

"It was the right moment."

"Even though you knew you would lose."

"At times you lose in order to win."

"More sentimentalism! In order to win in politics you've got to be *ready* to win. You've got to have the steely conviction of a Lenin who was willing to work as a German agent and cross Germany in a sealed train – because the moment in Russia was ripe for him."

"In other words, if you want to win, be a Castro."

"Yeah! Be a Castro!"

"But I'm not willing."

"And that's why you'll never win."

"I don't buy that," Emi retorted. "I think the universe is moved by forces much more powerful than those of a Castro. They're not as obvious, and they take more time to mature; but they have time on their side and they will prevail. *That's* the sealed train in which I travel."

Adolfo, reclining on the bed, took off his glasses. He was choking with emotion, tears pouring down his face. He turned to Emi and said: "I asked them to shoot you."

A flock of images went rushing through Emi's mind. In the last of them, he was at his trial and *la vieja* was whispering to him: "Your brother says you should not speak a word."

For 27 years Emi had been angered by that advice. Above all, he understood that his brother did not want him to make a scene in court; that Adolfo feared a public scene by Emi would damage his own good standing in the Communist Party.

In the midst of Emi's misfortune, Adolfo's move had reeked of opportunism. From politics and history, Emi had learned that communists are natural opportunists. Like the basest *bourgeois*, they will sacrifice almost any value for the sake of scoring high in appearances.

In his own character, Emi had forged the strongest possible aversion to opportunism. He had staked his life, with nearly two decades of prison, on his hatred of it. And he was keenly sensitive to the traces of opportunism in his brother's behavior. Whenever Emi thought of Adolfo's advice at the trial, he feared the worst about his brother's character.

What he now saw in his brother's confession was that Adolfo was no opportunist at all.

I was deeply moved. I went to Adolfito and embraced and kissed him repeatedly. "No, no, no!" I exclaimed. "By telling them to shoot me, you saved my life! You saved my life!"

Adolfo was dumbstruck by his brother, as he had been ten thousand times before.

Emi, however, was roaring with delight.

"Listen, Adolfito! If you had wavered or pleaded for my life, they would have executed me to discipline you. If I had begged for mercy, they would have killed me out of contempt. Or If I had bargained with them, they would have emptied me and then killed me out of spite. But I didn't play their game. Neither did you. Your friend Blanco was right. We had something. They didn't understand it but they wanted it. So they didn't kill me and they didn't kill you. Because you and I, the two of us together, had something they wanted."

Adolfo was still mute.

"Look. If my system had been the one in power and you had been the one to be arrested, I would have asked for your life to be spared because in my system it would be natural. And it would be just as natural for my superiors to consider my request with favor. In your system, the main value is not compassion but selflessness. The cause comes before everything – even before your family. It's not nice, but it has nobility. I respect it. Maybe that's why your comrades respected me. They hated me. But they respected me."

Adolfo kept up a stony silence.

"In recommending that I be executed, you showed yourself to be a very pure man. Your comrades loved you for it. They couldn't help themselves. And it's a contradiction because communists are not supposed to act from love. But they do because they're human, and because it's unavoidable. I believe that the most powerful force in the world is love. And whatever the Party leaders might say about it, whatever reason they give, it was out of their love for you that they spared my life!"

Adolfo's silence broke. "You know what I'm thinking about?"

"What?"

"Something *los viejos* used to say – which they would say again if they could see us now. 'God writes straight with crooked lines.'"

Adolfo paused for a moment and said: "You and I have never gone in for that kind of stuff. But it meant a lot to them."

Listening to Adolfito, I was confirmed in the respect I had always had for him – for his self-denial, his honesty, his purity. That day in Paris, I felt I had never loved him so much.

Epilogue

Americans

Emi Rivero was not someone you expected to meet in Washington, DC. He had stepped from the pages of a Dostoyevsky novel. Like one of those characters who are just waiting to talk, he was eager to bare his soul and ready to have you bare yours.

By the time I met him, 1989, Emi had been in the United States for ten years. His life's work was making political trouble for Fidel Castro. In a perfect world he would have followed that vocation as an official of America's "deep state." But the world is not perfect, and the most pervasive quality of the deep state is its lack of depth.

Emi had served the US government – the CIA in particular – with utmost distinction. At times that kind of record will only buy you grief. So it was with Emi. In response to the perennial and somewhat graceless question from others – "What do you do?" – Emi did not have a pat reply. It was one of his most sympathetic qualities.

A short time after our meeting, I heard from our mutual friend[112] that Emi was looking for a place to live. That friend, who knew I was living by myself in a nine-room house, wondered whether I might take Emi in as a boarder.

Emi's arrival began a new chapter in my life. When he moved in, the Cuban revolution and its phenomenal cast of characters came with him.

Shortly after Emi joined me, his younger brother arrived from Paris and rented a room in the DC suburb of Arlington, very near my house. Unlike Emi who reached out freely to others, Adolfo was taciturn and private. I left him alone, and we became the best of friends.

Emi's epithet in Washington, as constant as the wine-dark sea, was 'the ex-political prisoner.' When I asked how much time he

---

[112] Andy Schmookler, author and political activist

had spent in jail, I expected to hear something like a year or two. In a level tone Emi said: "Eighteen-and-a-half years."

The brothers had made their mark in a society whose conflicts were livelier and more dangerous than most Americans realized. At local meetings they talked eloquently about matters that were vital to US security. All the while, our national discussions on those themes were at a grade-school level. The disparity was troubling.

The CIA's discreet blacklisting of Emi didn't keep him from helping his brother. Thanks to Emi's advocacy Adolfo got a job at Radio Martí, the State Department's Cuba broadcaster, and later at *el Nuevo Herald*, Miami's major Spanish-language newspaper.

In the US Adolfo gave up the last vestiges of his communist belief and reinvented himself as a political conservative. His columns and broadcasts became a staple among Spanish-language audiences. As the Internet matured, he established www.neoliberalismo.com on which he published his own translations of pieces by American political thinkers.[113]

Emi eked out a living as a freelance teacher and translator. His passion was to work at tracking Fidel's activities. The 'maximum leader' was exporting subversion to all corners of the hemisphere, while nearly all of America's political experts looked the other way. Emi busied himself as a policy wonk and as an occasional activist on Capitol Hill, where he cut a notable figure with his old-world gallantry and style.

By far my favorite pastimes with Emi and Adolfo were the road-

---

[113] Since Adolfo's death, various friends have maintained the website with Adolfo's work at the center of it. Adolfo's translations include selections from the works of Thomas Sowell, Charles Krauthammer, David Horowitz, and Victor Davis Hanson. Emi also had a Web presence that others have kept alive since his passing. His writings, at www.newcubacoalition.org/, are in four languages including the German and Russian he learned as a prisoner.

trips we took between Arlington and Miami. I had decided to write a book about their experiences. In Miami I interviewed many of their friends; on the drives I interviewed the brothers themselves.

Those road-trips played a crucial role in my research. The story of the Rivero family was not the stuff of easygoing banter. It was a rough-and-tumble saga that posed many obstacles in the telling. Like people everywhere who have dealt with civil strife and repression, added to the complexities of 'normal' life, Cubans do not talk easily about their struggles. The stories that mean most to them are the ones they keep locked inside.

So it happens that Cuba's history is rendered in euphemisms or evasions that allow the various parties to tell their stories without really telling them. For each brother and me to get to the center of things, we needed the desolate hours of those long drives to let the awkward silences do their work and push out the truth.

Even with all the hard-won details woven into a careful manuscript, the story found no public audience. When I submitted the work to prospective publishers, they gave it a cold shoulder. Several friends kept copies of the manuscript and at times reminded me of it.

Twenty-odd years down the road, Emi and Adolfo had died in obscurity while their nemesis was carried away on wings of glory, with elegies that turned his most reckless deeds into accomplishments.[114] I for my part was holding a unique narrative that had become an inheritance. Once again, it was time to pick up the pen on this subject.

---

[114] According to the obituary in *The New York Times*, Castro was "the fiery apostle of revolution who brought the Cold War to the Western Hemisphere in 1959 and then defied the United States for nearly half a century as Cuba's maximum leader, bedeviling 11 American presidents and briefly pushing the world to the brink of nuclear war . . ." https://www.nytimes.com/2016/11/26/world/americas/fidel-castro-dies.html

§§§

The lives of Emi and Adolfo have a curious analogue in the game of *jai alai*. In 1962 Castro's regime closed all commercial *jai alai* courts in Cuba. The exciting game of wagers was economically incorrect in a socialist order. More basically the 'merry festival' – as *jai alai* means in Basque, its native tongue – ran against the grain of revolutionary morality.

After being kicked out of Cuba, *jai alai* went into decline throughout the Americas. Paradoxically, shrinking opportunities toughened the play and produced a higher level of performance. In 2013 a Miami manager could assert: "Some of the best *jai alai* ever played is being played right now. And almost nobody's around to see it."[115]

Adolfo and Emi both lived to see the second decade of the 21st century. Their troubles had turned them into stronger men. In their later years they were at the top of their game. Almost nobody was around to see that, either.

The Cuba they knew and loved had ceased to exist. But like their parents before them, the brothers had fully realized the promise of America. In their case, America's bounty was not fame or money but freedom and security.

For the Rivero brothers, America was also the country of the future. Their mature activism, which took root in American soil, had a strikingly youthful air. They woke up every day with the idea that the best of humanity, and the best of themselves, lay ahead.

In May 2011, at age 75, Adolfo succumbed to cancer as had both his parents. In January 2016, at age 87, Emi was on his way to the

---

[115] https://www.sbnation.com/longform/2013/2/28/4036934/jai-alai-sport-in-america-miami

National Press Club – his favorite haunt in Washington – when he took a fall and struck his head fatally.

Decades earlier, when he was drowning in the Florida Straits, Emi had told himself: "What a stupid way to die!"

What then is a smart way to die? The smart way is to leave nothing undone. Adolfo and Emi left nothing undone.

The legacy of the Rivero brothers is a simple thought which permeates the family history like sunlight filtering through trees. The ordinary, decent humans of this world are in constant peril from forces like the ones that haunted the Riveros. But the qualities on display in that family will prevail against any effort, no matter how skillful or determined, to take one's humanity away.

INDEX

Brothers from Time to Time is a relatively short work of history, divided into 70 chapters and an epilogue. In its print format, most chapters do not have more than one or two page-turns. So the text is measured by chapters, not pages; and terms are here located by chapter numbers.

People are listed by how they are called in the narrative. Usually that's by first name, and that includes two heads of state. First is the omnipresent 'Fidel.' Second is 'Nikita,' rather easier to pronounce than 'Khrushchev.'

Terms

Aníbal Escalante

Cienfuegos, Camilo, Rebel army *comandante*, 11
"Clock Radio" (*Radio Reloj*), popular Havana broadcaster, 5
Coca-Cola, American soft drink, symbol of US imperium, 62
Combinado del Este, major prison in Havana, 59, 64-67

A great many people think of Cuba as an island, beginning with Cubans themselves who call their country "the island." But Cuba is an archipelago with more than 4,000 islands; the topical map at the start of Chapter 34 shows the two largest of those.

Fidel Castro

Plinio Prieto

Prison, political under Castro

65; Adolfo spends five months in the lockup of State Security, another of Emi's former residences, 67-68; Emi & Adolfo relate their experiences as a vindication of their principles, 70

'Prisoners of chance,' bad-luck cases in Cuba's political prisons, 43

CHAPTERS
Part One: Regimes

Part Three: Trials

Part Four: Victories

Emi & Adolfo, Paris, May 1988

- -

Emi & Adolfo flanking the author, 1989